Regular Expression
Pocket Reference

Regular Expression
Pocket Reference

Tony Stubblebine

Beijing · Cambridge · Farnham · Köln · Paris · Sebastopol · Taipei · Tokyo

Regular Expression Pocket Reference
by Tony Stubblebine

Published by O'Reilly Media, Inc., 1005 Gravenstein Highway North,
Sebastopol, CA 95472.

O'Reilly Media, Inc. books may be purchased for educational,
business, or sales promotional use. Online editions are also available
for most titles (*safari.oreilly.com*). For more information, contact our
corporate/institutional sales department: (800) 998-9938 or
corporate@oreilly.com.

Editor:	Nathan Torkington
Production Editor:	Genevieve d'Entremont
Cover Designer:	Hanna Dyer
Interior Designer:	David Futato

Printing History:

August 2003:   First Edition.

ISBN-10: 0-596-00415-X
ISBN-13: 978-0-596-00415-6
[C]

Contents

Regular Expression Pocket Reference

Regular expressions (known as regexps or regexes) are a way to describe text through pattern matching. You might want to use regular expressions to validate data, to pull pieces of text out of larger blocks, or to substitute new text for old text.

Regular expression syntax defines a language you use to describe text. Today, regular expressions are included in most programming languages as well as many scripting languages, editors, applications, databases, and command-line tools. This book aims to give quick access to the syntax and pattern-matching operations of the most popular of these languages.

About This Book

This book starts with a general introduction to regular expressions. The first section of this book describes and defines the constructs used in regular expressions and establishes the common principles of pattern matching. The remaining sections of the book are devoted to the syntax, features, and usage of regular expressions in various implementations.

The implementations covered in this book are Perl, Java, .NET and C#, Python, PCRE, PHP, the *vi* editor, JavaScript, and shell tools.

Conventions Used in This Book

The following typographical conventions are used in this book:

Italic

> Used for emphasis, new terms, program names, and URLs

Constant width

> Used for options, values, code fragments, and any text that should be typed literally

Constant width italic

> Used for text that should be replaced with user-supplied values

Acknowledgments

The world of regular expressions is complex and filled with nuance. Jeffrey Friedl has written the definitive work on the subject, *Mastering Regular Expressions* (O'Reilly), a work on which I relied heavily when writing this book. As a convenience, this book provides page references to *Mastering Regular Expressions*, Second Edition (MRE) for expanded discussion of regular expression syntax and concepts.

This book simply would not have been written if Jeffrey Friedl had not blazed a trail ahead of me. Additionally, I owe him many thanks for allowing me to reuse the structure of his book and for his suggestions on improving this book. Nat Torkington's early guidance raised the bar for this book. Philip Hazel, Ron Hitchens, A.M. Kuchling, and Brad Merrill reviewed individual chapters. Linda Mui saved my sanity and this book. Tim Allwine's constant regex questions helped me solidify my knowledge of this topic. Thanks to Schuyler Erle and David Lents for letting me bounce ideas off of them. Lastly, many thanks to Sarah Burcham for her contributions to the "Shell Tools" sections and for providing the inspiration and opportunity to work and write for O'Reilly.

Introduction to Regexes and Pattern Matching

A *regular expression* is a string containing a combination of normal characters and special metacharacters or metasequences. The normal characters match themselves. *Metacharacters* and *metasequences* are characters or sequences of characters that represent ideas such as quantity, locations, or types of characters. The list in the section "Regex Metacharacters, Modes, and Constructs" shows the most common metacharacters and metasequences in the regular expression world. Later sections list the availability of and syntax for supported metacharacters for particular implementations of regular expressions.

Pattern matching consists of finding a section of text that is described (matched) by a regular expression. The underlying code that searchs the text is the *regular expression engine*. You can guess the results of most matches by keeping two rules in mind:

1. *The earliest (leftmost) match wins*

   Regular expressions are applied to the input starting at the first character and proceeding toward the last. As soon as the regular expression engine finds a match, it returns. (See MRE 148-149, 177–179.)

2. *Standard quantifiers are greedy*

   Quantifiers specify how many times something can be repeated. The standard quantifiers attempt to match as many times as possible. They settle for less than the maximum only if this is necessary for the success of the match. The process of giving up characters and trying less-greedy matches is called backtracking. (See MRE 151–153.)

Regular expression engines have subtle differences based on their type. There are two classes of engines: Deterministic Finite Automaton (DFA) and Nondeterministic Finite Automaton (NFA). DFAs are faster but lack many of the features of an NFA, such as capturing, lookaround, and non-greedy quantifiers. In the NFA world there are two types: Traditional and POSIX.

DFA engines

DFAs compare each character of the input string to the regular expression, keeping track of all matches in progress. Since each character is examined at most once, the DFA engine is the fastest. One additional rule to remember with DFAs is that the alternation metasequence is greedy. When more than one option in an alternation (foo|foobar) matches, the longest one is selected. So, rule #1 can be amended to read "the longest leftmost match wins." (See MRE 155–156.)

Traditional NFA engines

Traditional NFA engines compare each element of the regex to the input string, keeping track of positions where it chose between two options in the regex. If an option fails, the engine backtracks to the most recently saved position. For standard quantifiers, the engine chooses the greedy option of matching more text; however, if that option leads to the failure of the match, the engine returns to a saved position and tries a less greedy path. The traditional NFA engine uses ordered alternation, where each option in the alternation is tried sequentially. A longer match may be ignored if an earlier option leads to a successful match. So, rule #1 can be amended to read "the first leftmost match after greedy quantifiers have had their fill." (See MRE 153–154.)

POSIX NFA engines

POSIX NFA Engines work similarly to Traditional NFAs with one exception: a POSIX engine always picks the longest of the leftmost matches. For example, the alternation cat|category would match the full word "category" whenever possible, even if the first alternative ("cat") matched and appeared earlier in the alternation. (See MRE 153–154.)

Regex Metacharacters, Modes, and Constructs

The metacharacters and metasequences shown here represent most available types of regular expression constructs and their most common syntax. However, syntax and availability vary by implementation.

Character representations

Many implementations provide shortcuts to represent some characters that may be difficult to input. (See MRE 114–117.)

Character shorthands

Most implementations have specific shorthands for the alert, backspace, escape character, form feed, newline, carriage return, horizontal tab, and vertical tab characters. For example, \n is often a shorthand for the newline character, which is usually LF (012 octal) but can sometimes be CR (15 octal) depending on the operating system. Confusingly, many implementations use \b to mean both backspace and word boundary (between a "word" character and a non-word character). For these implementations, \b means backspace in a character class (a set of possible characters to match in the string) and word boundary elsewhere.

Octal escape: \num

Represents a character corresponding to a two- or three-octal digit number. For example, \015\012 matches an ASCII CR/LF sequence.

Hex and Unicode escapes: \xnum, \x{num}, \unum, \Unum

Represents a character corresponding to a hexadecimal number. Four-digit and larger hex numbers can represent the range of Unicode characters. For example, \x0D\x0A matches an ASCII CR/LF sequence.

Control characters: \c*char*

Corresponds to ASCII control characters encoded with values less than 32. To be safe, always use an uppercase *char*—some implementations do not handle lowercase representations. For example, \cH matches Control-H, an ASCII backspace character.

Character classes and class-like constructs

Character classes are ways to define or specify a set of characters. A character class matches one character in the input string that is within the defined set. (See MRE 117–127.)

Normal classes: [...] *and* [^...]

Character classes, [...], and negated character classes, [^...], allow you to list the characters that you do or do not want to match. A character class always matches one character. The - (dash) indicates a range of characters. To include the dash in the list of characters, list it first or escape it. For example, [a-z] matches any lowercase ASCII letter.

Almost any character: dot (.)

Usually matches any character except a newline. The match mode can often be changed so that dot also matches newlines.

Class shorthands: \w, \d, \s, \W, \D, \S

Commonly provided shorthands for word character, digit, and space character classes. A *word character* is often all ASCII alphanumeric characters plus the underscore. However, the list of alphanumerics can include additional locale or Unicode alphanumerics, depending on the implementation. For example, \d matches a single digit character and is usually equivalent to [0-9].

POSIX character class: [:*alnum*:]

POSIX defines several character classes that can be used only within regular expression character classes (see Table 1). For example, [:lower:], when written as [[:lower:]], is equivalent to [a-z] in the ASCII locale.

Unicode properties, scripts, and blocks: `\p{prop}`, `\P{prop}`

The Unicode standard defines classes of characters that have a particular property, belong to a script, or exist within a block. *Properties* are characteristics such as being a letter or a number (see Table 2). *Scripts* are systems of writing, such as Hebrew, Latin, or Han. *Blocks* are ranges of characters on the Unicode character map. Some implementations require that Unicode properties be prefixed with `Is` or `In`. For example, `\p{Ll}` matches lowercase letters in any Unicode supported language, such as a or α.

Unicode combining character sequence: `\X`

Matches a Unicode base character followed by any number of Unicode combining characters. This is a shorthand for `\P{M}\p{M}`. For example, `\X` matches è as well as the two characters e`'`.

Table 1. POSIX character classes

Class	Meaning
alnum	Letters and digits.
alpha	Letters.
blank	Space or tab only.
cntrl	Control characters.
digit	Decimal digits.
graph	Printing characters, excluding space.
lower	Lowercase letters.
print	Printing characters, including space.
punct	Printing characters, excluding letters and digits.
space	Whitespace.
upper	Uppercase letters.
xdigit	Hexadecimal digits.

Table 2. Standard Unicode properties

Property	Meaning
\p{L}	Letters.
\p{Ll}	Lowercase letters.
\p{Lm}	Modifier letters.
\p{Lo}	Letters, other. These have no case and are not considered modifiers.
\p{Lt}	Titlecase letters.
\p{Lu}	Uppercase letters.
\p{C}	Control codes and characters not in other categories.
\p{Cc}	ASCII and Latin-1 control characters.
\p{Cf}	Non-visible formatting characters.
\p{Cn}	Unassigned code points.
\p{Co}	Private use, such as company logos.
\p{Cs}	Surrogates.
\p{M}	Marks meant to combine with base characters, such as accent marks.
\p{Mc}	Modification characters that take up their own space. Examples include "vowel signs."
\p{Me}	Marks that enclose other characters, such as circles, squares, and diamonds.
\p{Mn}	Characters that modify other characters, such as accents and umlauts.
\p{N}	Numeric characters.
\p{Nd}	Decimal digits in various scripts.
\p{Nl}	Letters that are numbers, such as Roman numerals.
\p{No}	Superscripts, symbols, or non-digit characters representing numbers.
\p{P}	Punctuation.
\p{Pc}	Connecting punctuation, such as an underscore.
\p{Pd}	Dashes and hyphens.
\p{Pe}	Closing punctuation complementing \p{Ps}.
\p{Pi}	Initial punctuation, such as opening quotes.
\p{Pf}	Final punctuation, such as closing quotes.
\p{Po}	Other punctuation marks.
\p{Ps}	Opening punctuation, such as opening parentheses.

Table 2. Standard Unicode properties (continued)

Property	Meaning
\p{S}	Symbols.
\p{Sc}	Currency.
\p{Sk}	Combining characters represented as individual characters.
\p{Sm}	Math symbols.
\p{So}	Other symbols.
\p{Z}	Separating characters with no visual representation.
\p{Zl}	Line separators.
\p{Zp}	Paragraph separators.
\p{Zs}	Space characters.

Anchors and zero-width assertions

Anchors and "zero-width assertions" match positions in the input string. (See MRE 127–133.)

Start of line/string: ^, \A

Matches at the beginning of the text being searched. In multiline mode, ^ matches after any newline. Some implementations support \A, which only matches at the beginning of the text.

End of line/string: $, \Z, \z

$ matches at the end of a string. Some implementations also allow $ to match before a string-ending newline. If modified by multiline mode, $ matches before any newline as well. When supported, \Z matches the end of string or before a string-ending newline, regardless of match mode. Some implementations also provide \z, which only matches the end of the string, regardless of newlines.

Start of match: \G

In iterative matching, \G matches the position where the previous match ended. Often, this spot is reset to the beginning of a string on a failed match.

Word boundary: \b, \B, \<, \>

Word boundary metacharacters match a location where a word character is next to a non-word character. \b often specifies a word boundary location, and \B often specifies a not-word-boundary location. Some implementations provide separate metasequences for start- and end-of-word boundaries, often \< and \>.

Lookahead: (?=...), (?!...)
Lookbehind: (?<=...), (?<!...)

Lookaround constructs match a location in the text where the subpattern would match (lookahead), would not match (negative lookahead), would have finished matching (lookbehind), or would not have finished matching (negative lookbehind). For example, foo(?=bar) matches foo in foobar but not food. Implementations often limit lookbehind constructs to subpatterns with a predetermined length.

Comments and mode modifiers

Mode modifiers are a way to change how the regular expression engine interprets a regular expression. (See MRE 109–112, 133–135.)

Multiline mode: m

Changes the behavior of ^ and $ to match next to newlines within the input string.

Single-line mode: s

Changes the behavior of . (dot) to match all characters, including newlines, within the input string.

Case-insensitive mode: i

Treat as identical letters that differ only in case.

Free-spacing mode: x

Allows for whitespace and comments within a regular expression. The whitespace and comments (starting with # and extending to the end of the line) are ignored by the regular expression engine.

Mode modifiers: (?i), (?-i), (?*mod*:…)

Usually, mode modifiers may be set within a regular expression with (?*mod*) to turn modes on for the rest of the current subexpression; (?-*mod*) to turn modes off for the rest of the current subexpression; and (?*mod*:...) to turn modes on or off between the colon and the closing parentheses. For example, "use (?i:perl)" matches "use perl", "use Perl", "use PeRl", etc.

Comments: (?#...) *and* #

In free-spacing mode, # indicates that the rest of the line is a comment. When supported, the comment span (?#...) can be embedded anywhere in a regular expression, regardless of mode. For example, .{0,80}(?#Field limit is 80 chars) allows you to make notes about why you wrote .{0,80}.

Literal-text span: \Q...\E

Escapes metacharacters between \Q and \E. For example, \Q(.*)\E is the same as \(\.*\).

Grouping, capturing, conditionals, and control

This section covers the syntax for grouping subpatterns, capturing submatches, conditional submatches, and quantifying the number of times a subpattern matches. (See MRE 135–140.)

Capturing and grouping parentheses: (...) *and* \1, \2, ...

Parentheses perform two functions: grouping and capturing. Text matched by the subpattern within parentheses is captured for later use. Capturing parentheses are numbered by counting their opening parentheses from the left. If backreferences are available, the submatch can be referred to later in the same match with \1, \2, etc. The captured text is made available after a match by implementation-specific methods. For example, \b(\w+)\b\s+\1\b matches duplicate words, such as the the.

Grouping-only parentheses: (?:...)

Groups a subexpression, possibly for alternation or quantifiers, but does not capture the submatch. This is useful for efficiency and reusability. For example, (?:foobar) matches foobar, but does not save the match to a capture group.

Named capture: (?<name>...)

Performs capturing and grouping, with captured text later referenced by *name*. For example, Subject: (?<subject>.*) captures the text following Subject: to a capture group that can be referenced by the name subject.

Atomic grouping: (?>...)

Text matched within the group is never backtracked into, even if this leads to a match failure. For example, (?>[ab]*)\w\w matches aabbcc but not aabbaa.

Alternation: ...|...

Allows several subexpressions to be tested. Alternation's low precedence sometimes causes subexpressions to be longer than intended, so use parentheses to specifically group what you want alternated. For example, \b(foo|bar)\b matches either of the words foo or bar.

Conditional: (?if then | else)

The *if* is implementation dependent, but generally is a reference to a captured subexpression or a lookaround. The *then* and *else* parts are both regular expression patterns. If the *if* part is true, the *then* is applied. Otherwise, *else* is applied. For example, (<)?foo(?(1)>|bar) matches <foo> and foobar.

Greedy quantifiers: *, +, ?, {num,num }

The greedy quantifiers determine how many times a construct may be applied. They attempt to match as many times as possible, but will backtrack and give up matches if necessary for the success of the overall match. For example, (ab)+ matches all of abababab.

Lazy quantifiers: *?, +?, ??, {*num,num* }?

> Lazy quantifiers control how many times a construct may be applied. However, unlike greedy quantifiers, they attempt to match as few times as possible. For example, (an)+? matches only an of banana.

Possessive Quantifiers: *+, ++, ?+, {*num,num* }+

> Possessive quantifiers are like greedy quantifiers, except that they "lock in" their match, disallowing later backtracking to break up the sub-match. For example, (ab)++ab will not match abababab.

Unicode Support

Unicode is a character set that gives unique numbers to the characters in all the world's languages. Because of the large number of possible characters, Unicode requires more than one byte to represent a character. Some regular expression implementations will not understand Unicode characters, because they expect one-byte ASCII characters. Basic support for Unicode characters starts with being able to match a literal string of Unicode characters. Advanced support includes character classes and other constructs that contain characters from all Unicode-supported languages. For example, \w might match è as well as e.

Perl 5.8

Perl provides a rich set of regular-expression operators, constructs, and features, with more being added in each new release. Perl uses a Traditional NFA match engine. For an explanation of the rules behind an NFA engine, see "Introduction to Regexes and Pattern Matching."

This reference covers Perl Version 5.8. Unicode features were introduced in 5.6, but did not stabilize until 5.8. Most other features work in Versions 5.004 and later.

Supported Metacharacters

Perl supports the metacharacters and metasequences listed in Tables 3 through 7. For expanded definitions of each metacharacter, see "Regex Metacharacters, Modes, and Constructs."

Table 3. Character representations

Sequence	Meaning
\a	Alert (bell).
\b	Backspace; supported only in character class.
\e	ESC character, x1B.
\n	Newline; x0A on Unix and Windows, x0D on Mac OS 9.
\r	Carriage return; x0D on Unix and Windows, x0A on Mac OS 9.
\f	Form feed, x0C.
\t	Horizontal tab, x09.
\octal	Character specified by a two- or three-digit octal code.
\xhex	Character specified by a one- or two-digit hexadecimal code.
\x{hex}	Character specified by any hexadecimal code.
\cchar	Named control character.
\N{name}	A named character specified in the Unicode standard or listed in PATH_TO_PERLLIB/unicode/Names.txt. Requires use charnames ':full'.

Table 4. Character classes and class-like constructs

Class	Meaning
[...]	A single character listed or contained in a listed range.
[^...]	A single character not listed and not contained within a listed range.
[:class:]	POSIX-style character class valid only within a regex character class.
.	Any character except newline (unless single-line mode, /s).
\C	One byte; however, this may corrupt a Unicode character stream.
\X	Base character followed by any number of Unicode combining characters.

Table 4. Character classes and class-like constructs (continued)

Class	Meaning
\w	Word character, \p{IsWord}.
\W	Non-word character ,\P{IsWord}.
\d	Digit character, \p{IsDigit}.
\D	Non-digit character, \P{IsDigit}.
\s	Whitespace character, \p{IsSpace}.
\S	Non-whitespace character, \P{IsSpace}.
\p{*prop*}	Character contained by given Unicode property, script, or block.
\P{*prop*}	Character not contained by given Unicode property, script, or block.

Table 5. Anchors and zero-width tests

Sequence	Meaning
^	Start of string, or after any newline in multiline match mode, /m.
\A	Start of search string, in all match modes.
$	End of search string or before a string-ending newline, or before any newline in multiline match mode, /m.
\Z	End of string or before a string-ending newline, in any match mode.
\z	End of string, in any match mode.
\G	Beginning of current search.
\b	Word boundary.
\B	Not-word-boundary.
(?=...)	Positive lookahead.
(?!...)	Negative lookahead.
(?<=...)	Positive lookbehind; fixed-length only.
(?<!...)	Negative lookbehind; fixed-length only.

Table 6. Comments and mode modifiers

Modifier	Meaning
/i	Case-insensitive matching.
/m	^ and $ match next to embedded \n.

Table 6. Comments and mode modifiers (continued)

Modifier	Meaning
/s	Dot (.) matches newline.
/x	Ignore whitespace and allow comments (#) in pattern.
/o	Compile pattern only once.
(?mode)	Turn listed modes (xsmi) on for the rest of the subexpression.
(?-mode)	Turn listed modes (xsmi) off for the rest of the subexpression.
(?mode:...)	Turn listed modes (xsmi) on within parentheses.
(?-mode:...)	Turn listed modes (xsmi) off within parentheses.
(?#...)	Treat substring as a comment.
#...	Treat rest of line as a comment in /x mode.
\u	Force next character to uppercase.
\l	Force next character to lowercase.
\U	Force all following characters to uppercase.
\L	Force all following characters to lowercase.
\Q	Quote all following regex metacharacters.
\E	End a span started with \U, \L, or \Q.

Table 7. Grouping, capturing, conditional, and control

Sequence	Meaning
(...)	Group subpattern and capture submatch into \1,\2,... and $1, $2,....
\n	Contains text matched by the nth capture group.
(?:...)	Groups subpattern, but does not capture submatch.
(?>...)	Disallow backtracking for text matched by subpattern.
...|...	Try subpatterns in alternation.
*	Match 0 or more times.
+	Match 1 or more times.
?	Match 1 or 0 times.
{n}	Match exactly n times.
{n,}	Match at least n times.

Table 7. Grouping, capturing, conditional, and control (continued)

Sequence	Meaning
{x,y}	Match at least x times but no more than y times.
*?	Match 0 or more times, but as few times as possible.
+?	Match 1 or more times, but as few times as possible.
??	Match 0 or 1 time, but as few times as possible.
{n,}?	Match at least n times, but as few times as possible.
{x,y}?	Match at least x times, no more than y times, but as few times as possible .
(?(COND)...|...)	Match with if-then-else pattern where COND is an integer referring to either a backreference or a lookaround assertion.
(?(COND)...)	Match with if-then pattern.
(?{CODE})	Execute embedded Perl code.
(??{CODE})	Match regex from embedded Perl code.

Regular Expression Operators

Perl provides the built-in regular expression operators qr//, m//, and s///, as well as the split function. Each operator accepts a regular expression pattern string that is run through string and variable interpolation and then compiled.

Regular expressions are often delimited with the forward slash, but you can pick any non-alphanumeric, non-whitespace character. Here are some examples:

```
qr#...#        m!...!        m{...}
s|...|...|     s[...][...]   s<...>/.../
```

A match delimited by slashes (/.../) doesn't require a leading m:

```
/.../      #same as m/.../
```

Using the single quote as a delimiter suppresses interpolation of variables and the constructs \N{*name*}, \u, \l, \U, \L, \Q, \E. Normally these are interpolated before being passed to the regular expression engine.

qr// (Quote Regex)

qr/*PATTERN*/ismxo

Quote and compile *PATTERN* as a regular expression. The returned value may be used in a later pattern match or substitution. This saves time if the regular expression is going to be repeatedly interpolated. The match modes (or lack of), /ismxo, are locked in.

m// (Matching)

m/*PATTERN*/imsxocg

Match *PATTERN* against input string. In list context, returns a list of substrings matched by capturing parentheses, or else (1) for a successful match or ( ) for a failed match. In scalar context, returns 1 for success or "" for failure. /imsxo are optional mode modifiers. /cg are optional match modifiers. /g in scalar context causes the match to start from the end of the previous match. In list context, a /g match returns all matches or all captured substrings from all matches. A failed /g match will reset the match start to the beginning of the string unless the match is in combined /cg mode.

s/// (Substitution)

s/*PATTERN*/*REPLACEMENT*/egimosx

Match *PATTERN* in the input string and replace the match text with *REPLACEMENT*, returning the number of successes. /imosx are optional mode modifiers. /g substitutes all occurrences of *PATTERN*. Each /e causes an evaluation of *REPLACEMENT* as Perl code.

split

```
split /PATTERN/, EXPR, LIMIT
split /PATTERN/, EXPR
split /PATTERN/
split
```

Return a list of substrings surrounding matches of *PATTERN* in *EXPR*. If *LIMIT*, the list contains substrings surrounding the first *LIMIT* matches. The pattern argument is a match operator, so use m if you want alternate delimiters (e.g., split m{*PATTERN*}). The match permits the same modifiers as m{}. Table 8 lists the after-match variables.

Table 8. After-match variables

Variable	Meaning
$1, $2, ...	Captured submatches.
@-	$-[0] offset of start of match. $-[*n*] offset of start of $*n*.
@+	$+[0] offset of end of match. $+[*n*] offset of end of $*n*.
$+	Last parenthesized match.
$`	Text before match. Causes all regular expressions to be slower. Same as substr($input, 0, $-[0]).
$&	Text of match. Causes all regular expressions to be slower. Same as substr($input, $-[0], $+[0] - $-[0]).
$'	Text after match. Causes all regular expressions to be slower. Same as substr($input, $+[0]).
$^N	Text of most recently closed capturing parentheses.
$*	If true, /m is assumed for all matches without a /s.
$^R	The result value of the most recently executed code construct within a pattern match.

Unicode Support

Perl provides built-in support for Unicode 3.2, including full support in the \w, \d, \s, and \b metasequences.

The following constructs respect the current locale if use locale is defined: case-insensitive (i) mode, \L, \l, \U, \u, \w, and \W.

Perl supports the standard Unicode properties (see Table 2) as well as Perl-specific composite properties (see Table 9). Scripts and properties may have an Is prefix but do not require it. Blocks require an In prefix only if the block name conflicts with a script name.

Table 9. Composite Unicode properties

Property	Equivalent
IsASCII	[\x00-\x7f]
IsAlnum	[\p{Ll}\p{Lu}\p{Lt}\p{Lo}\p{Nd}]

Table 9. Composite Unicode properties (continued)

Property	Equivalent
IsAlpha	[\p{Ll}\p{Lu}\p{Lt}\p{Lo}]
IsCntrl	\p{C}
IsDigit	\p{Nd}
IsGraph	[^\p{C}\p{Space}]
IsLower	\p{Ll}
IsPrint	\P{C}
IsPunct	\p{P}
IsSpace	[\t\n\f\r\p{Z}]
IsUppper	[\p{Lu}\p{Lt}]
IsWord	[_\p{Ll}\p{Lu}\p{Lt}\p{Lo}\p{Nd}]
IsXDigit	[0-9a-fA-F]

Examples

Example 1. Simple match

```
# Match Spider-Man, Spiderman, SPIDER-MAN, etc.
my $dailybugle = "Spider-Man Menaces City!";
if ($dailybugle =~ m/spider[- ]?man/i) { do_something(); }
```

Example 2. Match, capture group, and qr

```
# Match dates formatted like MM/DD/YYYY, MM-DD-YY,...
my $date  = "12/30/1969";
my $regex = qr!(\d\d)[-/](\d\d)[-/](\d\d(?:\d\d)?)!;
if ($date =~ m/$regex/) {
  print "Day= ", $1,
        "Month=", $2,
        "Year= ", $3;
}
```

Example 3. Simple substitution

```
# Convert <br> to <br /> for XHTML compliance
my $text = "Hello World! <br>";
$text =~ s#<br>#<br />#ig;
```

Example 4. Harder substitution

```
# urlify - turn URL's into HTML links
$text = "Check the website, http://www.oreilly.com/catalog/
regexppr.";
$text =~
    s{
        \b                          # start at word boundary
        (                           # capture to $1
          (https?|telnet|gopher|file|wais|ftp) :
                                    # resource and colon
          [\w/#~:.?+=&%@!\-] +?      # one or more valid
                                    # characters
                                    # but take as little as
                                    # possible
        )
        (?=                         # lookahead
          [.:?\-] *                 #  for possible punctuation
          (?: [^\w/#~:.?+=&%@!\-]    #  invalid character
            | $ )                   #  or end of string
        )
    }{<a href="$1">$1</a>}igox;
```

Other Resources

- *Programming Perl*, by Larry Wall, Tom Christiansen, and Jon Orwant (O'Reilly), is the standard Perl reference.

- *Mastering Regular Expressions*, Second Edition, by Jeffrey E. F. Friedl (O'Reilly), covers the details of Perl regular expressions on pages 283–364.

- *perlre* is the perldoc documentation provided with most Perl distributions.

Java (java.util.regex)

Java 1.4 supports regular expressions with Sun's java.util. regex package. Although there are competing packages available for previous versions of Java, Sun is poised to become the standard. Sun's package uses a Traditional NFA match engine. For an explanation of the rules behind a Traditional NFA engine, see "Introduction to Regexes and Pattern Matching."

Supported Metacharacters

`java.util.regex` supports the metacharacters and metasequences listed in Tables 10 through 14. For expanded definitions of each metacharacter, see "Regex Metacharacters, Modes, and Constructs."

Table 10. Character representations

Sequence	Meaning
\a	Alert (bell).
\b	Backspace, x08, supported only in character class.
\e	ESC character, x1B.
\n	Newline, x0A.
\r	Carriage return, x0D.
\f	Form feed, x0C.
\t	Horizontal tab, x09.
\0*octal*	Character specified by a one-, two-, or three-digit octal code.
\x*hex*	Character specified by a two-digit hexadecimal code.
\u*hex*	Unicode character specified by a four-digit hexadecimal code.
\c*char*	Named control character.

Table 11. Character classes and class-like constructs

Class	Meaning
[...]	A single character listed or contained in a listed range.
[^...]	A single character not listed and not contained within a listed range.
.	Any character, except a line terminator (unless DOTALL mode).
\w	Word character, [a-zA-Z0-9_].
\W	Non-word character, [^a-zA-Z0-9_].
\d	Digit, [0-9].
\D	Non-digit, [^0-9].
\s	Whitespace character, [\t\n\f\r\x0B].
\S	Non-whitespace character, [^ \t\n\f\r\x0B].

Table 11. Character classes and class-like constructs (continued)

Class	Meaning
\p{*prop*}	Character contained by given POSIX character class, Unicode property, or Unicode block.
\P{*prop*}	Character not contained by given POSIX character class, Unicode property, or Unicode block.

Table 12. Anchors and other zero-width tests

Sequence	Meaning
^	Start of string, or after any newline if in MULTILINE mode.
\A	Beginning of string, in any match mode.
$	End of string, or before any newline if in MULTILINE mode.
\Z	End of string but before any final line terminator, in any match mode.
\z	End of string, in any match mode.
\b	Word boundary.
\B	Not-word-boundary.
\G	Beginning of current search.
(?=...)	Positive lookahead.
(?!...)	Negative lookahead.
(?<=...)	Positive lookbehind.
(?<!...)	Negative lookbehind.

Table 13. Comments and mode modifiers

Modifier/sequence	Mode character	Meaning
Pattern.UNIX_LINES	d	Treat \n as the only line terminator.
Pattern.DOTALL	s	Dot (.) matches any character, including a line terminator.
Pattern.MULTILINE	m	^ and $ match next to embedded line terminators.
Pattern.COMMENTS	x	Ignore whitespace and allow embedded comments starting with #.

Table 13. Comments and mode modifiers (continued)

Modifier/sequence	Mode character	Meaning
Pattern.CASE_ INSENSITIVE	i	Case-insensitive match for ASCII characters.
Pattern.UNICODE_ CASE	u	Case-insensitive match for Unicode characters.
Pattern.CANON_EQ		Unicode "canonical equivalence" mode where characters or sequences of a base character and combining characters with identical visual representations are treated as equals.
(?mode)		Turn listed modes (idmsux) on for the rest of the subexpression.
(?-mode)		Turn listed modes (idmsux) off for the rest of the subexpression.
(?mode:...)		Turn listed modes (idmsux) on within parentheses.
(?-mode:...)		Turn listed modes (idmsux) off within parentheses.
#...		Treat rest of line as a comment in /x mode.

Table 14. Grouping, capturing, conditional, and control

Sequence	Meaning
(...)	Group subpattern and capture submatch into \1,\2,... and $1, $2,....
\n	Contains text matched by the *n*th capture group.
$n	In a replacement string, contains text matched by the *n*th capture group.
(?:...)	Groups subpattern, but does not capture submatch.
(?>...)	Disallow backtracking for text matched by subpattern.
...|...	Try subpatterns in alternation.
*	Match 0 or more times.
+	Match 1 or more times.
?	Match 1 or 0 times.

Table 14. Grouping, capturing, conditional, and control (continued)

Sequence	Meaning
{*n*}	Match exactly *n* times.
{*n*,}	Match at least *n* times.
{*x,y*}	Match at least *x* times, but no more than *y* times.
*?	Match 0 or more times, but as few times as possible.
+?	Match 1 or more times, but as few times as possible.
??	Match 0 or 1 times, but as few times as possible.
{*n*,}?	Match at least *n* times, but as few times as possible.
{*x,y*}?	Match at least *x* times, no more than *y* times, and as few times as possible.
*+	Match 0 or more times, and never backtrack.
++	Match 1 or more times, and never backtrack.
?+	Match 0 or 1 times, and never backtrack.
{*n*}+	Match at least *n* times, and never backtrack.
{*n*,}+	Match at least *n* times, and never backtrack.
{*x,y*}+	Match at least *x* times, no more than *y* times, and never backtrack.

Regular Expression Classes and Interfaces

Java 1.4 introduces two main classes, java.util.regex. Pattern and java.util.regex.Matcher; an exception, java. util.regex.PatternSyntaxException; and a new interface, CharSequence. Additionally, Sun upgraded the String class to implement the CharSequence interface and to provide basic pattern-matching methods. Pattern objects are compiled regular expressions that can be applied to many strings. A Matcher object is a match of one Pattern applied to one string (or any object implementing CharSequence).

Backslashes in regular expression String literals need to be escaped. So \n (newline) becomes \\n when used in a Java String literal that is to be used as a regular expression.

java.lang.String

Description
New methods for pattern matching.

Methods
boolean matches (String *regex*)
> Return true if *regex* matches the entire String.

String[ ] split (String *regex*)
> Return an array of the substrings surrounding matches of *regex*.

String [ ] split (String *regex*, int *limit*)
> Return an array of the substrings surrounding the first *limit*-1 matches of *regex*.

String replaceFirst (String *regex*, String *replacement*)
> Replace the substring matched by *regex* with *replacement*.

String replaceAll (String *regex*, String *replacement*)
> Replace all substrings matched by *regex* with *replacement*.

---

java.util.regex.Pattern extends Object and implements Serializable

Description
Models a regular expression pattern.

Methods
static Pattern compile(String *regex*)
> Construct a Pattern object from *regex*.

static Pattern compile(String *regex*, int *flags*)
> Construct a new Pattern object out of *regex* and the OR'd mode-modifier constants *flags*.

int flags( )
> Return the Pattern's mode modifiers.

Matcher matcher(CharSequence *input*)
> Construct a Matcher object that will match this Pattern against *input*.

static boolean matches(String *regex*, CharSequence *input*)
> Return true if *regex* matches the entire string *input*.

```
String pattern( )
```
Return the regular expression used to create this Pattern.

```
String[ ] split(CharSequence input)
```
Return an array of the substrings surrounding matches of this Pattern in *input*.

```
String[ ] split(CharSequence input, int limit)
```
Return an array of the substrings surrounding the first *limit* matches of this pattern in *regex*.

java.util.regex.Matcher

extends Object

Description

Models a regular expression pattern matcher and pattern matching results.

Methods

```
Matcher appendReplacement(StringBuffer sb, String
    replacement)
```
Append substring preceding match and *replacement* to *sb*.

```
StringBuffer appendTail(StringBuffer sb)
```
Appends substring following end of match to *sb*.

```
int end( )
```
Index of the first character after the end of the match.

```
int end(int group)
```
Index of the first character after the text captured by *group*.

```
boolean find( )
```
Find the next match in the input string.

```
boolean find(int start)
```
Find the next match after character position, *start*.

```
String group( )
```
Text matched by this Pattern.

```
String group(int group)
```
Text captured by capture group, *group*.

```
int groupCount( )
```
Number of capturing groups in Pattern.

```
boolean lookingAt( )
```
True if match is at beginning of input.

```
boolean matches( )
```
Return true if Pattern matches entire input string.

```
Pattern pattern( )
```
Return Pattern object used by this Matcher.

```
String replaceAll(String replacement)
```
Replace every match with *replacement*.

```
String replaceFirst(String replacement)
```
Replace first match with *replacement*.

```
Matcher reset( )
```
Reset this matcher so that the next match starts at the beginning of the input string.

```
Matcher reset(CharSequence input)
```
Reset this matcher with new *input*.

```
int start( )
```
Index of first character matched.

```
int start(int group)
```
Index of first character matched in captured substring, *group*.

---

java.util.regex.PatternSyntaxException implements Serializable

Description

Thrown to indicate a syntax error in a regular expression pattern.

Methods

```
PatternSyntaxException(String desc, String regex, int index)
```
Construct an instance of this class.

```
String getDescription( )
```
Return error description.

```
int getIndex( )
```
Return error index.

```
String getMessage( )
```
Return a multiline error message containing error description, index, regular expression pattern, and indication of the position of the error within the pattern.

```
String getPattern( )
```
Return the regular expression pattern that threw the exception.

Description

Defines an interface for read-only access so that regular expression patterns may be applied to a sequence of characters.

Methods

char charAt(int *index*)
    Return the character at the zero-based position, *index*.

int length( )
    Return the number of characters in the sequence.

CharSequence subSequence(int *start*, int *end*)
    Return a subsequence including the *start* index and excluding the *end* index.

String toString( )
    Return a String representation of the sequence.

Unicode Support

This package supports Unicode 3.0, although \w, \W, \d, \D, \s, and \S support only ASCII. You can use the equivalent Unicode properties \p{L}, \P{L}, \p{Nd}, \P{Nd}, \p{Z}, and \P{Z}. The word boundary sequences, \b and \B, do understand Unicode.

For supported Unicode properties and blocks, see Table 2. This package supports only the short property names, such as \p{Lu}, and not \p{Lowercase_Letter}. Block names require the In prefix and support only the name form without spaces or underscores; for example, \p{InGreekExtended}, not \p{In_Greek_Extended} or \p{In Greek Extended}.

Examples

Example 5. Simple match

```
//Match Spider-Man, Spiderman, SPIDER-MAN, etc.
public class StringRegexTest {
```

Example 5. Simple match (continued)

```java
  public static void main(String[] args) throws Exception {
    String dailybugle = "Spider-Man Menaces City!";

    //regex must match entire string
    String regex = "(?i).*spider[- ]?man.*";

    if (dailybugle.matches(regex)) {
      //do something
    }
  }
}
```

Example 6. Match and capture group

```java
//Match dates formatted like MM/DD/YYYY, MM-DD-YY,...
import java.util.regex.*;

public class MatchTest {
  public static void main(String[] args) throws Exception {
    String date = "12/30/1969";
    Pattern p =
      Pattern.compile("(\\d\\d)[-/](\\d\\d)[-/](\\d\\d(?:\\d\\
d)?)");

    Matcher m = p.matcher(date);

    if (m.find()) {
      String month = m.group(1);
      String day   = m.group(2);
      String year  = m.group(3);
    }
  }
}
```

Example 7. Simple substitution

```java
//Convert <br> to <br /> for XHTML compliance
import java.util.regex.*;

public class SimpleSubstitutionTest {
  public static void main(String[] args) {
    String text = "Hello world. <br>";
```

Example 7. Simple substitution (continued)

```
    try {
      Pattern p = Pattern.compile("<br>", Pattern.CASE_
INSENSITIVE);
      Matcher m = p.matcher(text);

      String result = m.replaceAll("<br />");
    }
    catch (PatternSyntaxException e) {
      System.out.println(e.getMessage( ));
    }
    catch (Exception e) { System.exit( ); }

  }

}
```

Example 8. Harder substitution

```
//urlify - turn URL's into HTML links
import java.util.regex.*;

public class Urlify {
  public static void main (String[ ] args) throws Exception {
    String text = "Check the website, http://www.oreilly.com/
catalog/regexppr.";
    String regex =
         "\\b                         # start at word\n"
    +    "                            # boundary\n"
    +    "(                           # capture to $1\n"
    +    "(https?|telnet|gopher|file|wais|ftp) : \n"
    +    "                            # resource and colon\n"
    +    "[\\w/\\#~:.?+=&%@!\\-] +?    # one or more valid\n"
    +    "                            # characters\n"
    +    "                            # but take as little\n"
    +    "                            # as possible\n"
    +    ")\n"
    +    "(?=                         # lookahead\n"
    +    "[.:?\\-] *                  # for possible punc\n"
    +    "(?: [^\\\\w/\\#~:.?+=&%@!\\-] # invalid character\n"
    +    "| $ )                       # or end of string\n"
    +    ")";
```

Example 8. Harder substitution (continued)

```
    Pattern p = Pattern.compile(regex,
        Pattern.CASE_INSENSITIVE + Pattern.COMMENTS);
    Matcher m = p.matcher(text);
    String result = m.replaceAll("<a href=\"$1\">$1</a>");
  }
}
```

Other Resources

- *Java NIO*, by Ron Hitchens (O'Reilly), shows regular expressions in the context of Java's new I/O improvements.
- *Mastering Regular Expressions*, Second Edition, by Jeffrey E. F. Friedl (O'Reilly), covers the details of Java regular expressions on pages 378–391.
- Sun's online documentation at *http://java.sun.com/j2se/1.4/docs/api/java/util/regex/package-summary.html*.

.NET and C#

Microsoft's .NET framework provides a consistent and powerful set of regular expression classes for all .NET implementations. The following sections list the .NET regular expression syntax, the core .NET classes, and C# examples. Microsoft's .NET uses a Traditional NFA match engine. For an explanation of the rules behind a Traditional NFA engine, see "Introduction to Regexes and Pattern Matching."

Supported Metacharacters

.NET supports the metacharacters and metasequences listed in Tables 15 through 20. For expanded definitions of each metacharacter, see "Regex Metacharacters, Modes, and Constructs."

Table 15. Character representations

Sequence	Meaning
\a	Alert (bell), x07.
\b	Backspace, x08, supported only in character class.
\e	ESC character, x1B.
\n	Newline, x0A.
\r	Carriage return, x0D.
\f	Form feed, x0C.
\t	Horizontal tab, x09.
\v	Vertical tab, x0B.
\0*octal*	Character specified by a two-digit octal code.
\x*hex*	Character specified by a two-digit hexadecimal code.
\u*hex*	Character specified by a four-digit hexadecimal code.
\c*char*	Named control character.

Table 16. Character classes and class-like constructs

Class	Meaning
[...]	A single character listed or contained within a listed range.
[^...]	A single character not listed and not contained within a listed range.
.	Any character, except a line terminator (unless single-line mode, s).
\w	Word character, [\p{Ll}\p{Lu}\p{Lt}\p{Lo}\p{Nd}\p{Pc}] or [a-zA-Z_0-9] in ECMAScript mode.
\W	Non-word character, [\p{Ll}\p{Lu}\p{Lt}\p{Lo}\p{Nd}\p{Pc}] or [^a-zA-Z_0-9] in ECMAScript mode.
\d	Digit, \p{Nd} or [0-9] in ECMAScript mode.
\D	Non-digit, \P{Nd} or [^0-9] in ECMAScript mode.
\s	Whitespace character, [\f\n\r\t\v\x85\p{Z}] or [\f\n\r\t\v] in ECMAScript mode.
\S	Non-whitespace character, [^ \f\n\r\t\v\x85\p{Z}] or [^ \f\n\r\t\v] in ECMAScript mode.
\p{*prop*}	Character contained by given Unicode block or property.
\P{*prop*}	Character not contained by given Unicode block or property.

Table 17. Anchors and other zero-width tests

Sequence	Meaning
^	Start of string, or after any newline if in MULTILINE mode.
\A	Beginning of string, in all match modes.
$	End of string, or before any newline if in MULTILINE mode.
\Z	End of string but before any final line terminator, in all match modes.
\z	End of string, in all match modes.
\b	Boundary between a \w character and a \W character.
\B	Not-word-boundary.
\G	End of the previous match.
(?=...)	Positive lookahead.
(?!...)	Negative lookahead.
(?<=...)	Positive lookbehind.
(?<!...)	Negative lookbehind.

Table 18. Comments and mode modifiers

Modifier/sequence	Mode character	Meaning
Singleline	s	Dot (.) matches any character, including a line terminator.
Multiline	m	^ and $ match next to embedded line terminators.
IgnorePatternWhitespace	x	Ignore whitespace and allow embedded comments starting with #.
IgnoreCase	i	Case-insensitive match based on characters in the current culture.
CultureInvariant	i	Culture-insensitive match.
ExplicitCapture	n	Allow named capture groups, but treat parentheses as non-capturing groups.
Compiled		Compile regular expression.
RightToLeft		Search from right to left, starting to the left of the start position.
ECMAScript		Enables ECMAScript compliance when used with IgnoreCase or Multiline.

Table 18. Comments and mode modifiers (continued)

Modifier/sequence	Mode character	Meaning
`(?imnsx-imnsx)`		Turn match flags on or off for rest of pattern.
`(?imnsx-imnsx:...)`		Turn match flags on or off for the rest of the subexpression.
`(?#...)`		Treat substring as a comment.
`#...`		Treat rest of line as a comment in /x mode.

Table 19. Grouping, capturing, conditional, and control

Sequence	Meaning
`(...)`	Grouping. Submatches fill \1,\2,... and $1, $2,....
`\n`	In a regular expression, match what was matched by the *n*th earlier submatch.
`$n`	In a replacement string, contains the *n*th earlier submatch.
`(?<name>...)`	Captures matched substring into group, *name*.
`(?:...)`	Grouping-only parentheses, no capturing.
`(?>...)`	Disallow backtracking for subpattern.
`...|...`	Alternation; match one or the other.
`*`	Match 0 or more times.
`+`	Match 1 or more times.
`?`	Match 1 or 0 times.
`{n}`	Match exactly *n* times.
`{n,}`	Match at least *n* times.
`{x,y}`	Match at least *x* times, but no more than *y* times.
`*?`	Match 0 or more times, but as few times as possible.
`+?`	Match 1 or more times, but as few times as possible.
`??`	Match 0 or 1 times, but as few times as possible.
`{n,}?`	Match at least *n* times, but as few times as possible.
`{x,y}?`	Match at least *x* times, no more than *y* times, but as few times as possible.

Table 20. Replacement sequences

Sequence	Meaning
$1, $2, ...	Captured submatches.
${name}	Matched text of a named capture group.
$`	Text before match.
$&	Text of match.
$'	Text after match.
$+	Last parenthesized match.
$_	Copy of original input string.

Regular Expression Classes and Interfaces

.NET defines its regular expression support in the System. Text.RegularExpressions module. The RegExp() constructor handles regular expression creation, and the rest of the RegExp methods handle pattern matching. The Groups and Match classes contain information about each match.

C#'s raw string syntax, @"", allows you to define regular expression patterns without having to escape embedded backslashes.

Regex

This class handles the creation of regular expressions and pattern matching. Several static methods allow for pattern matching without creating a RegExp object.

Methods

```
public Regex(string pattern)
public Regex(string pattern, RegexOptions options)
```
Return a regular expression object based on *pattern* and with the optional mode modifiers, *options*.

```
public static void CompileToAssembly(RegexCompilationInfo[ ]
  regexinfos, System.Reflection.AssemblyName assemblyname)
public static void CompileToAssembly(RegexCompilationInfo[ ]
  regexinfos, System.Reflection.AssemblyName assemblyname)
public static void CompileToAssembly(RegexCompilationInfo[ ]
  regexinfos, System.Reflection.AssemblyName assemblyname,
  System.Reflection.Emit.CustomAttributeBuilder[ ] attributes)
public static void CompileToAssembly(RegexCompilationInfo[ ]
  regexinfos, System.Reflection.AssemblyName assemblyname,
  System.Reflection.Emit.CustomAttributeBuilder[ ] attributes,
  string resourceFile)
```

Compile one or more Regex objects to an assembly. The *regexinfos* array describes the regular expressions to include. The assembly filename is *assemblyname*. The array *attributes* defines attributes for the assembly. *resourceFile* is the name of a Win32 resource file to include in the assembly.

```
public static string Escape(string str)
```

Return a string with all regular expression metacharacters, pound characters (#), and whitespace escaped.

```
public static bool IsMatch(string input, string pattern)
public static bool IsMatch(string input, string pattern,
  RegexOptions options)
public bool IsMatch(string input)
public bool IsMatch(string input, int startat)
```

Return the success of a single match against the input string *input*. Static versions of this method require the regular expression *pattern*. The *options* parameter allows for optional mode modifiers (OR'd together). The *startat* parameter defines a starting position in *input* to start matching.

```
public static Match Match(string input, string pattern)
public static Match Match(string input, string pattern,
  RegExpOptions options)
public Match Match(string input)
public Match Match(string input, int startat)
public Match Match(string input, int startat, int length)
```

Perform a single match against the input string *input* and return information about the match in a Match object. Static versions of this method require the regular expression *pattern*. The *options* parameter allows for optional mode modifiers

(OR'd together). The *startat* and *length* parameters define a starting position and the number of characters after the starting position to perform the match.

```
public static MatchCollection Matches(string input, string
    pattern)
public static MatchCollection Matches(string input, string
    pattern, RegExpOptions options)
public MatchCollection Matches(string input)
public MatchCollection Matches(string input, int startat)
```

Find all matches in the input string *input*, and return information about the matches in a MatchCollection object. Static versions of this method require the regular expression *pattern*. The *options* parameter allows for optional mode modifiers (OR'd together). The *startat* parameter defines a starting position in *input* to perform the match.

```
public static string Replace(string input, pattern,
    MatchEvaluator evaluator)
public static string Replace(string input, pattern,
    MatchEvaluator evaluator, RegexOptions options)
public static string Replace(string input, pattern, string
    replacement)
public static string Replace(string input, pattern, string
    replacement, RegexOptions options)
public string Replace(string input, MatchEvaluator evaluator)
public string Replace(string input, MatchEvaluator evaluator,
    int count)
public string Replace(string input, MatchEvaluator evaluator,
    int count, int startat)
public string Replace(string input, string replacement)
public string Replace(string input, string replacement, int
    count)
public string Replace(string input, string replacement, int
    count, int startat)
```

Return a string in which each match in *input* is replaced with either the evaluation of the *replacement* string or a call to a MatchEvaluator object. The string *replacement* can contain backreferences to captured text with the $*n* or ${*name*} syntax.

The *options* parameter allows for optional mode modifiers (OR'd together). The *count* parameter limits the number of replacements. The *startat* parameter defines a starting position in *input* to start the replacement.

```
public static string[ ] Split(string input, string pattern)
public static string[ ] Split(string input, string pattern,
  RegexOptions options)
public static string[ ] Split(string input)
public static string[ ] Split(string input, int count)
public static string[ ] Split(string input, int count, int
  startat)
```

Return an array of strings broken around matches of the regex pattern. If specified, no more than *count* strings are returned. You can specify a starting position in *input* with *startat*.

Match

Properties

`public bool Success`
Indicates whether the match was successful.

`public string Value`
Text of the match.

`public int Length`
Number of characters in the matched text.

`public int Index`
Zero-based character index of the start of the match.

`public GroupCollection Groups`
A GroupCollection object where Groups[0].value contains the text of the entire match, and each additional Groups element contains the text matched by a capture group.

Methods

`public Match NextMatch( )`
Return a Match object for the next match of the regex in the input string.

`public virtual string Result(string result)`
Return *result* with special replacement sequences replaced by values from the previous match.

`public static Match Synchronized(Match inner)`
Return a Match object identical to *inner*, except also safe for multithreaded use.

Group

Properties

`public bool Success`
    True if the group participated in the match.

`public string Value`
    Text captured by this group.

`public int Length`
    Number of characters captured by this group.

`public int Index`
    Zero-based character index of the start of the text captured by this group.

Unicode Support

.NET provides built-in support for Unicode 3.1, including full support in the \w, \d, and \s sequences. The range of characters matched can be limited to ASCII characters by turning on `ECMAScript` mode. Case-insensitive matching is limited to the characters of the current language defined in `Thread.CurrentCulture`, unless the `CultureInvariant` option is set.

.NET supports the standard Unicode properties (see Table 2) and blocks. Only the short form of property names are supported. Block names require the `Is` prefix and must use the simple name form, without spaces or underscores.

Examples

Example 9. Simple match

```
//Match Spider-Man, Spiderman, SPIDER-MAN, etc.
namespace Regex_PocketRef
{
  using System.Text.RegularExpressions;

  class SimpleMatchTest
  {
    static void Main( )
```

Example 9. Simple match (continued)

```
    {
      string dailybugle = "Spider-Man Menaces City!";

      string regex = "spider[- ]?man";

    if (Regex.IsMatch(dailybugle, regex, RegexOptions.
IgnoreCase)) {
      //do something
    }
  }
}
```

Example 10. Match and capture group

```
//Match dates formatted like MM/DD/YYYY, MM-DD-YY,...
using System.Text.RegularExpressions;

class MatchTest
{
  static void Main( )
  {
    string date = "12/30/1969";
    Regex r =
      new Regex( @"(\d\d)[-/](\d\d)[-/](\d\d(?:\d\d)?)" );

    Match m = r.Match(date);

    if (m.Success) {
      string month = m.Groups[1].Value;
      string day   = m.Groups[2].Value;
      string year  = m.Groups[3].Value;
    }
  }
}
```

Example 11. Simple substitution

```
//Convert <br> to <br /> for XHTML compliance
using System.Text.RegularExpressions;

class SimpleSubstitutionTest
{
  static void Main( )
  {
```

Example 11. Simple substitution (continued)

```
    string text = "Hello world. <br>";
    string regex = "<br>";
    string replacement = "<br />";

    string result =
       Regex.Replace(text, regex, replacement, RegexOptions.
IgnoreCase);
  }
}
```

Example 12. Harder substitution

```
//urlify - turn URL's into HTML links
using System.Text.RegularExpressions;

public class Urlify
{
  static Main ()
  {
   string text = "Check the website, http://www.oreilly.com/
catalog/regexppr.";
    string regex =
       @"\b                           # start at word boundary
       (                              # capture to $1
       (https?|telnet|gopher|file|wais|ftp) :
                                      # resource and colon
       [\w/#~:.?+=&%@!\-] +?          # one or more valid
                                      # characters
                                      # but take as little as
                                      # possible
       )
       (?=                            # lookahead
       [.:?\-] *                      # for possible
                                      # punctuation
       (?: [^\w/#~:.?+=&%@!\-]        # invalid character
       | $ )                          # or end of string
       )";

    Regex r = new Regex(regex,  RegexOptions.IgnoreCase
                    | RegexOptions.IgnorePatternWhitespace);
    string result = r.Replace(text, "<a href=\"$1\">$1</a>");
  }
}
```

Other Resources

- *Programming C#*, by Jesse Liberty (O'Reilly), gives a thorough introduction to C#, .NET, and regular expressions.

- *Mastering Regular Expressions*, Second Edition, by Jeffrey E. F. Friedl (O'Reilly), covers the details and failings of .NET regular expressions on pages 399–432.

- Microsoft's online documentation at *http://msdn.microsoft. com/library/default.asp?url=/library/en-us/cpgenref/html/ cpconregularexpressionslanguageelements.asp*.

Python

Python provides a rich, Perl-like regular expression syntax in the re module. The re module uses a Traditional NFA match engine. For an explanation of the rules behind an NFA engine, see "Introduction to Regexes and Pattern Matching."

This chapter covers the version of re included with Python 2.2, although the module has been available in similar form since Python 1.5.

Supported Metacharacters

The re module supports the metacharacters and metasequences listed in Tables 21 through 25. For expanded definitions of each metacharacter, see "Regex Metacharacters, Modes, and Constructs."

Table 21. Character representations

Sequence	Meaning
\a	Alert (bell), x07.
\b	Backspace, x08, supported only in character class.
\n	Newline, x0A.
\r	Carriage return, x0D.
\f	Form feed, x0C.

Table 21. Character representations (continued)

Sequence	Meaning
\t	Horizontal tab, x09.
\v	Vertical tab, x0B.
\octal	Character specified by up to three octal digits.
\xhh	Character specified by a two-digit hexadecimal code.
\uhhhh	Character specified by a four-digit hexadecimal code.
\Uhhhhhhhh	Character specified by an eight-digit hexadecimal code.

Table 22. Character classes and class-like constructs

Class	Meaning
[...]	Any character listed or contained within a listed range.
[^...]	Any character that is not listed and is not contained within a listed range.
.	Any character, except a newline (unless DOTALL mode).
\w	Word character, [a-zA-z0-9_] (unless LOCALE or UNICODE mode).
\W	Non-word character, [^a-zA-z0-9_] (unless LOCALE or UNICODE mode).
\d	Digit character, [0-9].
\D	Non-digit character, [^0-9].
\s	Whitespace character, [\t\n\r\f\v].
\S	Nonwhitespace character, [\t\n\r\f\v].

Table 23. Anchors and zero-width tests

Sequence	Meaning
^	Start of string, or after any newline if in MULTILINE match mode.
\A	Start of search string, in all match modes.
$	End of search string or before a string-ending newline, or before any newline in MULTILINE match mode.
\Z	End of string or before a string-ending newline, in any match mode.
\b	Word boundary.

Table 23. Anchors and zero-width tests (continued)

Sequence	Meaning
\B	Not-word-boundary.
(?=...)	Positive lookahead.
(?!...)	Negative lookahead.
(?<=...)	Positive lookbehind.
(?<!...)	Negative lookbehind.

Table 24. Comments and mode modifiers

Modifier/sequence	Mode character	Meaning
I or IGNORECASE	i	Case-insensitive matching.
L or LOCALE	L	Cause \w, \W, \b, and \B to use current locale's definition of alphanumeric.
M or MULTILINE or (?m)	m	^ and $ match next to embedded \n.
S or DOTALL or (?s)	s	Dot (.) matches newline.
U or UNICODE or (?u)	u	Cause \w, \W, \b, and \B to use Unicode definition of alphanumeric.
X or VERBOSE or (?x)	x	Ignore whitespace and allow comments (#) in pattern.
(?mode)		Turn listed modes (iLmsux) on for the entire regular expression.
(?#...)		Treat substring as a comment.
#...		Treat rest of line as a comment in VERBOSE mode.

Table 25. Grouping, capturing, conditional, and control

Sequence	Meaning
(...)	Group subpattern and capture submatch into \1,\2,...
(?P<name> ...)	Group subpattern and capture submatch into named capture group, *name*.
(?P=name)	Match text matched by earlier named capture group, *name*.
\n	Contains the results of the *n*th earlier submatch.

Table 25. Grouping, capturing, conditional, and control (continued)

Sequence	Meaning
`(?:...)`	Groups subpattern, but does not capture submatch.
`...|...`	Try subpatterns in alternation.
`*`	Match 0 or more times.
`+`	Match 1 or more times.
`?`	Match 1 or 0 times.
`{n}`	Match exactly *n* times.
`{x,y}`	Match at least *x* times but no more than *y* times.
`*?`	Match 0 or more times, but as few times as possible.
`+?`	Match 1 or more times, but as few times as possible.
`??`	Match 0 or 1 time, but as few times as possible.
`{x,y}?`	Match at least *x* times, no more than *y* times, and as few times as possible.

re Module Objects and Functions

The re module defines all regular expression functionality. Pattern matching is done directly through module functions, or patterns are compiled into regular expression objects that can be used for repeated pattern matching. Information about the match, including captured groups, is retrieved through match objects.

Python's raw string syntax, r'' or r"", allows you to specify regular expression patterns without having to escape embedded backslashes. The raw-string pattern, r'\n', is equivalent to the regular string pattern, '\\n'. Python also provides triple-quoted raw strings for multiline regular expressions: r'''text''' and r"""text""".

Module Functions

The re module defines the following functions and one exception.

compile(*pattern* [, *flags*])
    Return a regular expression object with the optional mode modifiers, *flags*.

match(*pattern, string* [, *flags*])
    Search for *pattern* at starting position of *string*, and return a match object or None if no match.

search(*pattern, string* [, *flags*])
    Search for *pattern* in *string*, and return a match object or None if no match.

split(*pattern, string* [, *maxsplit=0*])
    Split *string* on *pattern*. Limit the number of splits to *maxsplit*. Submatches from capturing parentheses are also returned.

sub(*pattern, repl, string* [, *count=0*])
    Return a string with all or up to *count* occurrences of *pattern* in *string* replaced with *repl*. *repl* may be either a string or a function that takes a match object argument.

subn(*pattern, repl, string* [, *count=0*])
    Perform sub( ) but return a tuple of the new string and the number of replacements.

findall(*pattern, string*)
    Return matches of *pattern* in *string*. If *pattern* has capturing groups, returns a list of submatches or a list of tuples of submatches.

finditer(*pattern, string*)
    Return an iterator over matches of *pattern* in *string*. For each match, the iterator returns a match object.

escape(*string*)
    Return string with alphanumerics backslashed so that *string* can be matched literally.

exception error
    Exception raised if an error occurs during compilation or matching. This is common if a string passed to a function is not a valid regular expression.

RegExp

Regular expression objects are created with the re.compile function.

flags
    Return the flags argument used when the object was compiled or 0.

groupindex
>   Return a dictionary that maps symbolic group names to group
>   numbers.

pattern
>   Return the pattern string used when the object was compiled.

match(*string* [, *pos* [, *endpos*]])
search(*string* [, *pos* [, *endpos*]])
split(*string* [, *maxsplit=0*])
sub(*repl*, *string* [, *count=0*])
subn(*repl*, *string* [, *count=0*])
findall(*string*)
>   Same as the re module functions, except pattern is implied.
>   *pos* and *endpos* give start and end string indexes for the match.

Match Objects

Match objects are created by the match and find functions.

pos
endpos
>   Value of pos or endpos passed to search or match.

re
>   The regular expression object whose match or search returned
>   this object.

string
>   String passed to match or search.

group([*g1*, *g2*, ...])
>   Return one or more submatches from capturing groups.
>   Groups may be either numbers corresponding to capturing
>   groups or strings corresponding to named capturing groups.
>   Group zero corresponds to the entire match. If no arguments
>   are provided, this function returns the entire match.
>   Capturing groups that did not match have a result of None.

groups([*default*])
>   Return a tuple of the results of all capturing groups. Groups
>   that did not match have the value None or *default*.

groupdict([*default*])
>   Return a dictionary of named capture groups, keyed by group
>   name. Groups that did not match have the value None or
>   *default*.

start([*group*])
: Index of start of substring matched by *group* (or start of entire matched string if no *group*).

end([*group*])
: Index of end of substring matched by *group* (or end of entire matched string if no *group*).

span([*group*])
: Return a tuple of starting and ending indexes of *group* (or matched string if no *group*).

expand([*template*])
: Return a string obtained by doing backslash substitution on *template*. Character escapes, numeric backreferences, and named backreferences are expanded.

lastgroup
: Name of the last matching capture group, or None if no match or if the group had no name.

lastindex
: Index of the last matching capture group, or None if no match.

Unicode Support

re provides limited Unicode support. Strings may contain Unicode characters, and individual Unicode characters can be specified with \u. Additionally, the UNICODE flag causes \w, \W, \b, and \B to recognize all Unicode alphanumerics. However, re does not provide support for matching Unicode properties, blocks, or categories.

Examples

Example 13. Simple match

```
#Match Spider-Man, Spiderman, SPIDER-MAN, etc.
import re

dailybugle = 'Spider-Man Menaces City!'
pattern    = r'spider[- ]?man.'

if re.match(pattern, dailybugle, re.IGNORECASE):
    print dailybugle
```

Example 14. Match and capture group

```
#Match dates formatted like MM/DD/YYYY, MM-DD-YY,...
import re

date = '12/30/1969'

regex = re.compile(r'(\d\d)[-/](\d\d)[-/](\d\d(?:\d\d)?)')

match = regex.match(date)

if match:
    month = match.group(1) #12
    day   = match.group(2) #30
    year  = match.group(3) #1969
```

Example 15. Simple substitution

```
#Convert <br> to <br /> for XHTML compliance
import re

text  = 'Hello world. <br>'
regex = re.compile(r'<br>', re.IGNORECASE);
repl  = r'<br />'

result = regex.sub(repl,text)
```

Example 16. Harder substitution

```
#urlify - turn URL's into HTML links
import re

text = 'Check the website, http://www.oreilly.com/catalog/
regexppr.'

pattern = r'''
     \b                          # start at word boundary
      (                          # capture to \1
      (https?|telnet|gopher|file|wais|ftp) :
                                 # resource and colon
      [\w/#~:.?+=&%@!\-] +?       # one or more valid chars
                                 # take little as possible
     )
      (?=                        # lookahead
      [.:?\-] *                  #  for possible punc
```

Example 16. Harder substitution (continued)

```
        (?: [^\w/#~:.?+=&%@!\-]      # invalid character
        | $ )                        # or end of string
        )'''

regex = re.compile(pattern,  re.IGNORECASE
                             + re.VERBOSE)

result = regex.sub(r'<a href="\1">\1</a>', text)
```

Other Resources

Python's online documentation at *http://www.python.org/doc/current/lib/module-re.html*.

PCRE Lib

The Perl Compatible Regular Expression (PCRE) library is a free-for-any-use, open source regular expression library developed by Philip Hazel. PCRE has been incorporated into PHP, Apache 2.0, KDE, Exim MTA, Analog, and Postfix. Users of those programs can use the supported metacharacters listed in Tables 26 through 30.

The PCRE library uses a Traditional NFA match engine. For an explanation of the rules behind an NFA engine, see "Introduction to Regexes and Pattern Matching."

This reference covers PCRE Version 4.0, which aims to emulate Perl 5.8–style regular expressions.

Supported Metacharacters

PCRE supports the metacharacters and metasequences listed in Tables 26 through 30. For expanded definitions of each metacharacter, see "Regex Metacharacters, Modes, and Constructs."

Table 26. Character representations

Sequence	Meaning
\a	Alert (bell), x07.
\b	Backspace, x08, supported only in character class.
\e	ESC character, x1B.
\n	Newline, x0A.
\r	Carriage return, x0D.
\f	Form feed, x0C.
\t	Horizontal tab, x09.
octal	Character specified by a three-digit octal code.
\x*hex*	Character specified by a one- or two-digit hexadecimal code.
\x{*hex*}	Character specified by any hexadecimal code.
\c*char*	Named control character.

Table 27. Character classes and class-like constructs

Class	Meaning
[...]	A single character listed or contained in a listed range.
[^...]	A single character not listed and not contained within a listed range.
[:*class*:]	POSIX-style character class valid only within a regex character class.
.	Any character except newline (unless single-line mode, /s).
\C	One byte; however, this may corrupt a Unicode character stream.
\w	Word character, [a-zA-z0-9_].
\W	Non-word character, [^a-zA-z0-9_].
\d	Digit character, [0-9].
\D	Non-digit character, [^0-9].
\s	Whitespace character, [\n\r\f\t].
\S	Non-whitespace character, [^\n\r\f\t].

Table 28. Anchors and zero-width tests

Sequence	Meaning
^	Start of string, or after any newline if in multiline match mode, /m.
\A	Start of search string, in all match modes.
$	End of search string or before a string-ending newline, or before any newline if in multiline match mode, /m.
\Z	End of string or before a string-ending newline, in any match mode.
\z	End of string, in any match mode.
\G	Beginning of current search.
\b	Word boundary; position between a word character (\w) and either a non-word character (\W), the start of the string, or the end of the string.
\B	Not-word-boundary.
(?=...)	Positive lookahead.
(?!...)	Negative lookahead.
(?<=...)	Positive lookbehind.
(?<!...)	Negative lookbehind.

Table 29. Comments and mode modifiers

Modifier/sequence	Mode character	Meaning
PCRE_CASELESS	i	Case-insensitive matching for characters with codepoints values less than 256.
PCRE_MULTILINE	m	^ and $ match next to embedded \n.
PCRE_DOTALL	s	Dot (.) matches newline.
PCRE_EXTENDED	x	Ignore whitespace and allow comments (#) in pattern.
PCRE_UNGREEDY	U	Reverse greediness of all quantifiers: * becomes non-greedy and *? becomes greedy.
PCRE_ANCHORED		Force match to start at the first position searched.

Table 29. Comments and mode modifiers (continued)

Modifier/sequence	Mode character	Meaning
PCRE_DOLLAR_ENDONLY		Force $ to match at only the end of a string instead of before a string ending with a newline. Overridden by multiline mode.
PCRE_NO_AUTO_CAPTURE		Disable capturing function of parentheses.
PCRE_UTF8		Treat regular expression and subject strings as strings of multibyte UTF-8 characters.
(?mode)		Turn listed modes (imsxU) on for the rest of the subexpression.
(?-mode)		Turn listed modes (imsxU) off for the rest of the subexpression.
(?mode:...)		Turn listed modes (xsmi) on within parentheses.
(?-mode:...)		Turn listed modes (xsmi) off within parentheses.
\Q		Quote all following regex metacharacters.
\E		End a span started with \Q.
(?#...)		Treat substring as a comment.
#...		Treat rest of line as a comment in PCRE_EXTENDED mode.

Table 30. Grouping, capturing, conditional, and control

Sequence	Meaning
(...)	Group subpattern and capture submatch into \1,\2,...
(?P<name>...)	Group subpattern and capture submatch into named capture group, *name*.
\n	Contains the results of the *n*th earlier submatch from a parentheses capture group or a named capture group.
(?:...)	Group subpattern, but do not capture submatch.
(?>...)	Disallow backtracking for text matched by subpattern.
...|...	Try subpatterns in alternation.
*	Match 0 or more times.

Table 30. Grouping, capturing, conditional, and control (continued)

Sequence	Meaning
+	Match 1 or more times.
?	Match 1 or 0 times.
{n}	Match exactly n times.
{n,}	Match at least n times.
{x,y}	Match at least x times, but no more than y times.
*?	Match 0 or more times, but as few times as possible.
+?	Match 1 or more times, but as few times as possible.
??	Match 0 or 1 time, but as few times as possible.
{n,}?	Match at least n times, but as few times as possible.
{x,y}?	Match at least x times, no more than y times, and as few times as possible.
*+	Match 0 or more times, and never backtrack.
++	Match 1 or more times, and never backtrack.
?+	Match 0 or 1 times, and never backtrack.
{n}+	Match at least n times, and never backtrack.
{n,}+	Match at least n times, and never backtrack.
{x,y}+	Match at least x times, no more than y times, and never backtrack.
(?(condition) ...|...)	Match with if-then-else pattern. The condition can be either the number of a capture group or a lookahead or lookbehind construct.
(?(condition) ...)	Match with if-then pattern. The condition can be either the number of a capture group or a lookahead or lookbehind construct.

PCRE API

Applications using PCRE should look for the API prototypes in pcre.h and include the actual library file, libpcre.a, by compiling with -lpcre.

Most functionality is contained in the functions pcre_ compile( ), which prepares a regular expression data structure, and pcre_exec( ), which performs the pattern matching.

You are responsible for freeing memory, although PCRE does provide pcre_free_substring() and pcre_free_substring_list() to help out.

PCRE API Synopsis

pcre *pcre_compile(const char *pattern, int options, const char **errptr, int *erroffset, const unsigned char *tableptr)

Compile *pattern* with optional mode modifiers *options* and optional locale tables *tableptr*, which are created with pcre_maketables(). Returns either a compiled regex or NULL with *errptr* pointing to an error message and *erroffset* pointing to the position in *pattern* where the error occurred.

int pcre_exec(const pcre *code, const pcre_extra *extra, const char *subject, int length, int startoffset, int options, int *ovector, int ovecsize)

Perform pattern matching with a compiled regular expression, *code*, and a supplied input string, *subject*, of length *length*. The results of a successful match are stored in *ovector*. The first and second elements of *ovector* contain the position of the first character in the overall match and the character following the end of the overall match. Each additional pair of elements, up to two thirds the length of *ovector*, contain the positions of the starting character and the character after capture group submatches. Optional parameters *options* contain mode modifiers, and *pcre_extra* contains the results of a call to pcre_study().

pcre_extra *pcre_study(const pcre *code, int options, const char **errptr)

Return information to speed up calls to pcre_exec() with *code*. There are currently no options, so *options* should always be zero. If an error occurred, *errptr* points to an error message.

int pcre_copy_named_substring(const pcre *code, const char *subject, int *ovector, int stringcount, const char *stringname, char *buffer, int buffersize)

Copy the substring matched by the named capture group *stringname* into *buffer*. *stringcount* is the number of substrings placed into *ovector*, usually the result returned by pcre_exec().

```
int pcre_copy_substring(const char *subject, int *ovector, int
    stringcount, int stringnumber, char *buffer, int buffersize)
```
Copy the substring matched by the numbered capture group *stringnumber* into *buffer*. *stringcount* is the number of substrings placed into *ovector*, usually the result returned by pcre_exec( ).

```
int pcre_get_named_substring(const pcre *code, const char
    *subject, int *ovector, int stringcount, const char
    *stringname, const char **stringptr)
```
Create a new string, pointed to by *stringptr*, containing the substring matched by the named capture group *stringname*. Returns the length of the substring. *stringcount* is the number of substrings placed into *ovector*, usually the result returned by pcre_exec( ).

```
int pcre_get_stringnumber(const pcre *code, const char *name)
```
Return the numbered capture group associated with the named capture group, *name*.

```
int pcre_get_substring(const char *subject, int *ovector, int
    stringcount, int stringnumber, const char **stringptr)
```
Create a new string, pointed to by *stringptr*, containing the substring matched by the numbered capture group *stringnumber*. Returns the length of the substring. *stringcount* is the number of substrings placed into *ovector*, usually the result returned by pcre_exec( ).

```
int pcre_get_substring_list(const char *subject, int *ovector,
    int stringcount, const char ***listptr)
```
Return a list of pointers, *listptr*, to all captured substrings.

```
void pcre_free_substring(const char *stringptr)
```
Free memory pointed to by *stringptr* and allocated by pcre_get_named_substring( ) or pcre_get_substring_list( ).

```
void pcre_free_substring_list(const char **stringptr)
```
Free memory pointed to by *stringptr* and allocated by pcre_get_substring_list( ).

```
const unsigned char *pcre_maketables(void)
```
Build character tables for the current locale.

```
int pcre_fullinfo(const pcre *code, const pcre_extra *extra,
    int what, void *where)
```
Place info on a regex specified by *what* into *where*. Available values for *what* are PCRE_INFO_BACKREFMAX, PCRE_INFO_CAPTURECOUNT, PCRE_INFO_FIRSTBYTE, PCRE_INFO_FIRSTTABLE,

PCRE_INFO_LASTLITERAL, PCRE_INFO_NAMECOUNT, PCRE_INFO_NAMEENTRYSIZE, PCRE_INFO_NAMETABLE, PCRE_INFO_OPTIONS, PCRE_INFO_SIZE, and PCRE_INFO_STUDYSIZE.

int pcre_config(int *what*, void **where*)
> Place the value of build-time options specified by *what* into *where*. Available values for *what* are PCRE_CONFIG_UTF8, PCRE_CONFIG_NEWLINE, PCRE_CONFIG_LINK_SIZE, PCRE_CONFIG_POSIX_MALLOC_THRESHOLD, and PCRE_CONFIG_MATCH_LIMIT.

char *pcre_version(void)
> Return a pointer to a string containing the PCRE version and release date.

void *(*pcre_malloc)(size_t)
> Entry point PCRE uses for malloc( ) calls.

void (*pcre_free)(void *)
> Entry point PCRE uses for pcre_free( ) calls.

int (*pcre_callout)(pcre_callout_block *)
> Can be set to a callout function that will be called during matches.

Unicode Support

PCRE provides basic Unicode support. When a pattern is compiled with the PCRE_UTF8 flag, the pattern will run on Unicode text. However, PCRE has no capability to recognize any properties of characters whose values are greater than 256.

PCRE determines case and the property of being a letter or digit based on a set of default tables. You can supply an alternate set of tables based on a different locale. For example:

```
setlocale(LC_CTYPE, "fr");
tables = pcre_maketables( );
re = pcre_compile(..., tables);
```

Examples

Examples 17 and 18 are adapted from an open source example written by Philip Hazel and copyright by the University of Cambridge, England.

Example 17. Simple match

```c
#include <stdio.h>
#include <string.h>
#include <pcre.h>

#define CAPTUREVECTORSIZE 30   /* should be a multiple of 3 */

int main(int argc, char **argv)
{
pcre *regex;
const char *error;
int erroffset;
int capturevector[CAPTUREVECTORSIZE];
int rc;

char *pattern = "spider[- ]?man";
char *text ="SPIDERMAN menaces city!";

/* Compile Regex */
regex = pcre_compile(
  pattern,
  PCRE_CASELESS,  /* OR'd mode modifiers */
  &error,         /* error message */
  &erroffset,     /* position in regex where error occurred */
  NULL);          /* use default locale */

/* Handle Errors */
if (regex == NULL)
  {
  printf("Compilation failed at offset %d: %s\n", erroffset,
         error);
  return 1;
  }

/* Try Match */
rc = pcre_exec(
  regex,    /* compiled regular expression */
  NULL,     /* optional results from pcre_study */
  text,     /* input string */
  (int)strlen(text), /* length of input string */
  0,        /* starting position in input string */
  0,        /* OR'd options */
  capturevector, /* holds results of capture groups */
```

Example 17. Simple match (continued)

```
  CAPTUREVECTORSIZE);

/* Handle Errors */
if (rc < 0)
  {
  switch(rc)
    {
    case PCRE_ERROR_NOMATCH: printf("No match\n"); break;
    default: printf("Matching error %d\n", rc); break;
    }
  return 1;
  }
return 0;
}
```

Example 18. Match and capture group

```
#include <stdio.h>
#include <string.h>
#include <pcre.h>

#define CAPTUREVECTORSIZE 30    /* should be a multiple of 3 */

int main(int argc, char **argv)
{
pcre *regex;
const char *error;
int erroffset;
int capturevector[CAPTUREVECTORSIZE];
int rc, i;

char *pattern = "(\\d\\d)[-/](\\d\\d)[-/](\\d\\d(?:\\d\\d)?)";
char *text ="12/30/1969";

/* Compile the Regex */
re = pcre_compile(
  pattern,
  PCRE_CASELESS, /* OR'd mode modifiers */
  &error,        /* error message */
  &erroffset,    /* position in regex where error occurred */
  NULL);         /* use default locale */
```

Example 18. Match and capture group (continued)

```c
/* Handle compilation errors */
if (re == NULL)
  {
  printf("Compilation failed at offset %d: %s\n",
         erroffset, error);
  return 1;
  }

rc = pcre_exec(
  regex,    /* compiled regular expression */
  NULL,     /* optional results from pcre_study */
  text,     /* input string */
  (int)strlen(text), /* length of input string */
  0,        /* starting position in input string */
  0,        /* OR'd options */
  capturevector, /* holds results of capture groups */
  CAPTUREVECTORSIZE);

/* Handle Match Errors */
if (rc < 0)
  {
  switch(rc)
    {
    case PCRE_ERROR_NOMATCH: printf("No match\n"); break;
    /*
    Handle other special cases if you like
    */
    default: printf("Matching error %d\n", rc); break;
    }
  return 1;
  }

/* Match succeded */

printf("Match succeeded\n");

/* Check for output vector for capture groups */
if (rc == 0)
  {
  rc = CAPTUREVECTORSIZE/3;
  printf("ovector only has room for %d captured substrings\n",
         rc - 1);
```

Example 18. Match and capture group (continued)

```
  }

/* Show capture groups */

for (i = 0; i < rc; i++)
  {
  char *substring_start = text + ovector[2*i];
  int substring_length = capturevector[2*i+1]
                         - capturevector[2*i];
  printf("%2d: %.*s\n", i, substring_length, substring_start);
  }

return 0;
}
```

Other Resources

The C source code and documentation for PCRE at *http://www.pcre.org*.

PHP

This reference covers PHP 4.3's Perl-style regular expression support contained within the preg routines. PHP also provides POSIX-style regular expressions, but these do not offer additional benefit in power or speed. The preg routines use a Traditional NFA match engine. For an explanation of the rules behind an NFA engine, see "Introduction to Regexes and Pattern Matching."

Supported Metacharacters

PHP supports the metacharacters and metasequences listed in Tables 31 through 35. For expanded definitions of each metacharacter, see "Regex Metacharacters, Modes, and Constructs."

Table 31. Character representations

Sequence	Meaning
\a	Alert (bell), x07.
\b	Backspace, x08, supported only in character class.
\e	ESC character, x1B.
\n	Newline, x0A.
\r	Carriage return, x0D.
\f	Form feed, x0C.
\t	Horizontal tab, x09
\octal	Character specified by a three-digit octal code.
\xhex	Character specified by a one- or two-digit hexadecimal code.
\x{hex}	Character specified by any hexadecimal code.
\cchar	Named control character.

Table 32. Character classes and class-like constructs

Class	Meaning
[...]	A single character listed or contained within a listed range.
[^...]	A single character not listed and not contained within a listed range.
[:class:]	POSIX-style character class valid only within a regex character class.
.	Any character except newline (unless single-line mode, /s).
\C	One byte; however, this may corrupt a Unicode character stream.
\w	Word character, [a-zA-z0-9_].
\W	Non-word character, [^a-zA-z0-9_].
\d	Digit character, [0-9].
\D	Non-digit character, [^0-9].
\s	Whitespace character, [\n\r\f\t].
\S	Non-whitespace character, [^\n\r\f\t].

Table 33. Anchors and zero-width tests

Sequence	Meaning
^	Start of string, or after any newline if in multiline match mode, /m.
\A	Start of search string, in all match modes.
$	End of search string or before a string-ending newline, or before any newline if in multiline match mode, /m.
\Z	End of string or before a string-ending newline, in any match mode.
\z	End of string, in any match mode.
\G	Beginning of current search.
\b	Word boundary; position between a word character (\w) and a non-word character (\W), the start of the string, or the end of the string.
\B	Not-word-boundary.
(?=...)	Positive lookahead.
(?!...)	Negative lookahead.
(?<=...)	Positive lookbehind.
(?<!...)	Negative lookbehind.

Table 34. Comments and mode modifiers

Modes	Meaning
i	Case-insensitive matching.
m	^ and $ match next to embedded \n.
s	Dot (.) matches newline.
x	Ignore whitespace and allow comments (#) in pattern.
U	Inverts greediness of all quantifiers: * becomes lazy and *? greedy.
A	Force match to start at search start in subject string.
D	Force $ to match end of string instead of before the string ending newline. Overridden by multiline mode.
u	Treat regular expression and subject strings as strings of multi-byte UTF-8 characters.
(?mode)	Turn listed modes (imsxU) on for the rest of the subexpression.

Table 34. Comments and mode modifiers (continued)

Modes	Meaning
(?-mode)	Turn listed modes (imsxU) off for the rest of the subexpression.
(?mode:...)	Turn mode (xsmi) on within parentheses.
(?-mode:...)	Turn mode (xsmi) off within parentheses.
(?#...)	Treat substring as a comment.
#...	Rest of line is treated as a comment in x mode.
\Q	Quotes all following regex metacharacters.
\E	Ends a span started with \Q.

Table 35. Grouping, capturing, conditional, and control

Sequence	Meaning
(...)	Group subpattern and capture submatch into \1,\2,...
(?P<name>...)	Group subpattern and capture submatch into named capture group, *name*.
\n	Contains the results of the *n*th earlier submatch from a parentheses capture group or a named capture group.
(?:...)	Groups subpattern, but does not capture submatch.
(?>...)	Disallow backtracking for text matched by subpattern.
...|...	Try subpatterns in alternation.
*	Match 0 or more times.
+	Match 1 or more times.
?	Match 1 or 0 times.
{n}	Match exactly *n* times.
{n,}	Match at least *n* times.
{x,y}	Match at least *x* times but no more than *y* times.
*?	Match 0 or more times, but as few times as possible.
+?	Match 1 or more times, but as few times as possible.
??	Match 0 or 1 time, but as few times as possible.
{n,}?	Match at least *n* times, but as few times as possible.
{x,y}?	Match at least *x* times, no more than *y* times, and as few times as possible.

Table 35. Grouping, capturing, conditional, and control (continued)

Sequence	Meaning
*+	Match 0 or more times, and never backtrack.
++	Match 1 or more times, and never backtrack.
?+	Match 0 or 1 times, and never backtrack.
{n}+	Match at least n times, and never backtrack.
{n,}+	Match at least n times, and never backtrack.
{x,y}+	Match at least x times, no more than y times, and never backtrack.
(?(condition) ...|...)	Match with if-then-else pattern. The condition can be either the number of a capture group or a lookahead or lookbehind construct.
(?(condition) ...)	Match with if-then pattern. The condition can be either the number of a capture group or a lookahead or lookbehind construct.

Pattern-Matching Functions

PHP provides several standalone functions for pattern matching. When creating regular expression strings, you need to escape embedded backslashes; otherwise, the backslash is interpreted in the string before being sent to the regular expression engine.

array preg_grep (string *pattern*, array *input*)

Return array containing every element of *input* matched by *pattern*.

int preg_match_all (string *pattern*, string *subject*, array *matches* [, int *flags*])

Search for all matches of *pattern* against *subject* and return the number of matches. The matched substrings are placed in the *matches* array. The first element of *matches* is an array containing the text of each full match. Each additional element *N* of *matches* is an array containing the *N*th capture group match for each full match. So matches[7][3] contains the text matches by the seventh capture group in the fourth match of *pattern* in *subject*.

The default ordering of *matches* can be set explicitly with the PREG_SET_ORDER flag. PREG_SET_ORDER sets a more intuitive ordering where each element of *matches* is an array corresponding to a match. The zero element of each array is the complete match, and each additional element corresponds to a capture group. The additional flag PREG_OFFSET_CAPTURE causes each array element containing a string to be replaced with a two-element array containing the same string and starting character position in *subject*.

int preg_match (string *pattern*, string *subject* [, array *matches* [, int *flags*]])

Return 1 if *pattern* matches in *subject*, otherwise return 0. If the *matches* array is provided, the matched substring is placed in matches[0] and any capture group matches are placed in subsequent elements. One allowed flag, PREG_OFFSET_CAPTURE, causes elements of *matches* to be replaced with a two-element array containing the matched string and starting character position of the match.

string preg_quote (string *str* [, string *delimiter*])

Return a *str* with all regular expression metacharacters escaped. Provide the *delimiter* parameter if you are using optional delimiters with your regular expression and need the delimiter escaped in *str*.

mixed preg_replace_callback (mixed *pattern*, callback *callback,* mixed *subject* [, int *limit*])

Return text of *subject* with every occurrence of *pattern* replaced with the results of *callback*. The callback should take one parameter, an array containing the matched text and any matches from capture groups. If provided, the function performs no more than *limit* replacements.

If *pattern* is an array, each element is replaced with *callback*. If *subject* is an array, the function iterates over each element.

```
mixed preg_replace (mixed pattern, mixed replacement, mixed
    subject [, int limit])
```
> Return text of *subject* with every occurrence of *pattern*
> replaced with *replacement*. If provided, the function per-
> forms no more than *limit* replacements. The replace-
> ment string may refer to the match or capture group
> matches with $n (preferred) or \n (deprecated). If *pattern*
> has the /e modifier, *replacement* is parsed for reference
> substitution and then executed as PHP code.
>
> If *pattern* is an array, then each element is replaced with
> *replacement* or, if *replacement* is an array, the corre-
> sponding element in *replacement*. If *subject* is an array,
> the function iterates over each element.

```
array preg_split (string pattern, string subject [, int
    limit [, int flags]])
```
> Return an array of strings broken around *pattern*. If
> specified, preg_split( ) returns no more than *limit* sub-
> strings. A *limit* of -1 is the same as "no limit," allowing
> you to set flags. Available flags are: PREG_SPLIT_NO_EMPTY,
> return only non-empty pieces; PREG_SPLIT_DELIM_CAPTURE,
> return captured submatches after each split substring;
> and PREG_SPLIT_OFFSET_CAPTURE, return an array of two-
> element arrays where the first element is the match and
> the second element is the offset of the match in *subject*.

Examples

Example 19. Simple match

```
//Match Spider-Man, Spiderman, SPIDER-MAN, etc.
$dailybugle = "Spider-Man Menaces City!";

$regex = "/spider[- ]?man/i";

if (preg_match($regex, $dailybugle)) {
    //do something
}
```

Example 20. Match and capture group

```php
//Match dates formatted like MM/DD/YYYY, MM-DD-YY,...
$date = "12/30/1969";
$p    = "!(\\d\\d)[-/](\\d\\d)[-/](\\d\\d(?:\\d\\d)?)!";

if (preg_match($p,$date,$matches) {
        $month = $matches[1];
        $day   = $matches[2];
        $year  = $matches[3];
}
```

Example 21. Simple substitution

```php
//Convert <br> to <br /> for XHTML compliance
$text = "Hello world. <br>";

$pattern = "{<br>}i";

echo preg_replace($pattern, "<br />", $text);
```

Example 22. Harder substitution

```php
//urlify - turn URL's into HTML links
$text = "Check the website, http://www.oreilly.com/catalog/
regexppr.";
$regex =
        "{ \\b                         # start at word\n"
     .  "                              # boundary\n"
     .  "(                             # capture to $1\n"
     .  "(https?|telnet|gopher|file|wais|ftp) : \n"
     .  "                              # resource and colon\n"
     .  "[\\w/\\#~:.?+=&%@!\\-]+?      # one or more valid\n"
     .  "                              # characters\n"
     .  "                              # but take as little as\n"
     .  "                              # possible\n"
     .  ")\n"
     .  "(?=                           # lookahead\n"
     .  "[.:?\\-]*                     # for possible punct\n"
     .  "(?:[^\\w/\\#~:.?+=&%@!\\-]    # invalid character\n"
     .  "|$)                           # or end of string\n"
     .  ") }x";


echo preg_replace($regex, "<a href=\"$1\">$1</a>", $text);
```

Other Resources

- PHP's online documentation at *http://www.php.net/pcre*.

vi Editor

The *vi* program is a popular text editor on all Unix systems, and *Vim* is a popular *vi* clone with expanded regular expression support. Both use a DFA match engine. For an explanation of the rules behind a DFA engine, see "Introduction to Regexes and Pattern Matching."

Supported Metacharacters

Tables 36 through 40 list the metacharacters and metasequences supported by *vi*. For expanded definitions of each metacharacter, see "Regex Metacharacters, Modes, and Constructs."

Table 36. Character representation

Sequence	Meaning
Vim only	
\b	Backspace, x08.
\e	ESC character, x1B.
\n	Newline, x0A.
\r	Carriage return, x0D.
\t	Horizontal tab, x09.

Table 37. Character classes and class-like constructs

Class	Meaning
[...]	Any character listed or contained within a listed range.
[^...]	Any character that is not listed or contained within a listed range.
[:*class*:]	POSIX-style character class valid only within a character class.
.	Any character except newline (unless /s mode).

Table 37. Character classes and class-like constructs (continued)

Class	Meaning
Vim only	
\w	Word character, [a-zA-z0-9_].
\W	Non-word character, [^a-zA-z0-9_].
\a	Letter character, [a-zA-z].
\A	Non-letter character, [^a-zA-z].
\h	Head of word character, [a-zA-z_].
\H	Not the head of a word character, [^a-zA-z_].
\d	Digit character, [0-9].
\D	Non-digit character, [^0-9].
\s	Whitespace character, [\t].
\S	Non-whitespace character, [^ \t].
\x	Hex digit, [a-fA-F0-9].
\X	Non-hex digit, [^a-fA-F0-9].
\o	Octal digit, [0-7].
\O	Non-octal digit, [^0-7].
\l	Lowercase letter, [a-z].
\L	Non-lowercase letter, [^a-z].
\u	Uppercase letter, [A-Z].
\U	Non-uppercase letter, [^A-Z].
\i	Identifier character defined by isident.
\I	Any non-digit identifier character.
\k	Keyword character defined by iskeyword, often set by language modes.
\K	Any non-digit keyword character.
\f	Filename character defined by isfname. Operating system dependent.

Table 37. Character classes and class-like constructs (continued)

Class	Meaning
\F	Any non-digit filename character.
\p	Printable character defined by isprint, usually x20-x7E.
\P	Any non-digit printable character.

Table 38. Anchors and zero-width tests

Sequence	Meaning
^	Start of a line when appearing first in a regular expression; otherwise, it matches itself.
$	End of a line when appearing last in a regular expression; otherwise, it matches itself.
\<	Beginning of word boundary, (i.e., a position between a punctuation or space character and a word character).
\>	End of word boundary.

Table 39. Mode modifiers

Modifier	Meaning
:set ic	Turns on case-insensitive mode for all searching and substitution.
:set noic	Turns off case-insensitive mode.
\u	Force next character in a replacement string to uppercase.
\l	Force next character in a replacement string to lowercase.
\U	Force all following characters in a replacement string to uppercase.
\L	Force all following characters in a replacement string to lowercase.
\E or \e	Ends a span started with \U or \L.

Table 40. Grouping, capturing, conditional, and control

Sequence	Meaning
\(...\)	Group subpattern and capture submatch into \1,\2,...
\n	Contains the results of the nth earlier submatch. Valid in both a regex pattern or a replacement string.

Table 40. Grouping, capturing, conditional, and control (continued)

Sequence	Meaning
&	Evaluates to the matched text when used in a replacement string.
*	Match 0 or more times.
Vim only	
\+	Match 1 or more times.
\=	Match 1 or 0 times.
\{n}	Match exactly n times.
\{n,}	Match at least n times.
\{,n}	Match at most n times.
\{x,y}	Match at least x times, but no more than y times.

Pattern Matching

Searching

/*pattern*
?*pattern*

Moves to the start of the next position in the file matched by *pattern*. A ?*pattern* searches backwards. A search can be repeated with the n (search forward) or N (search backwards) commands.

Substitution

:[*addr1*[,*addr2*]]s/*pattern*/*replacement*/[cgp]

Replace the text matched by *pattern* with *replacement* on every line in the address range. If no address range is given, the current line is used. Each address may be either a line number or a regular expression. If *addr1* is supplied, substitution will begin on that line number (or the first matching line) and continue until either the end of the file or the line indicated (or matched) by *addr2*. There are also a number of address shortcuts, which are described in the following tables.

Substitution options

Option	Meaning
c	Prompt before each substitution.
g	Replace all matches on a line.
p	Print line after substitution.

Address shortcuts

Address	Meaning
.	Current line.
$	Last line in file.
%	Entire file.
't	Position "t".
/...[/]	Next line matched by pattern.
?...[?]	Next previous line matched by pattern.
\/	Next line matched by the last search.
\?	Next previous line matched by the last search.
\&	Next line where the last substitution pattern matched.

Examples

Example 23. Simple search in vi

```
Find spider-man, Spider-Man, Spider Man
/[Ss]pider[- ][Mm]an
```

Example 24. Simple search in Vim

```
Find spider-man, Spider-Man, Spider Man, spiderman, SPIDER-MAN, etc.
:set ic
/spider[- ]\=man
```

Example 25. Simple substitution in vi

```
Globally convert <br> to <br /> for XHTML compliance.
:set ic
: % s/<br>/<br \/>/
```

Example 26. Simple substitution in Vim

```
Globally convert <br> to <br /> for XHTML compliance.
: % s/<br>/<br \/>/i
```

Example 27. Harder substitution in Vim

```
Urlify: Turn URLs into HTML links
: % s/\(https\=:\/\/[a-z_.\\w\/\\#~:?+=&;%@!-]*\)/< a href="\
1">\1<\/a>/ic
```

Other Resources

- *Learning the vi Editor*, by Linda Lamb and Arnold Robbins (O'Reilly), is a guide to the *vi* editor and popular *vi* clones.

- *http://www.geocities.com/volontir/*, by Oleg Raisky, is an overview of *Vim* regular expression syntax.

JavaScript

JavaScript introduced Perl-like regular expression support with Version 1.2. This reference covers Version 1.5 as defined by the ECMA standard. Supporting implementations include Microsoft Internet Explorer 5.5+ and Netscape Navigator 6+. JavaScript uses a Traditional NFA match engine. For an explanation of the rules behind an NFA engine, see "Introduction to Regexes and Pattern Matching."

Supported Metacharacters

JavaScript supports the metacharacters and metasequences listed in Tables 41 through 45. For expanded definitions of each metacharacter, see "Regex Metacharacters, Modes, and Constructs."

Table 41. Character representations

Sequence	Meaning
\0	Null character, \x00.
\b	Backspace, \x08, supported only in character class.

Table 41. Character representations (continued)

Sequence	Meaning
\n	Newline, \x0A.
\r	Carriage return, \x0D.
\f	Form feed, \x0C.
\t	Horizontal tab, \x09.
\t	Vertical tab, \x0B.
\xhh	Character specified by a two-digit hexadecimal code.
\uhhhh	Character specified by a four-digit hexadecimal code.
\cchar	Named control character.

Table 42. Character classes and class-like constructs

Class	Meaning
[...]	A single character listed or contained within a listed range.
[^...]	A single character not listed and not contained within a listed range.
.	Any character except a line terminator, [^\x0A\x0D\u2028\u2029].
\w	Word character, [a-zA-Z0-9_].
\W	Non-word character, [^a-zA-Z0-9_].
\d	Digit character, [0-9].
\D	Non-digit character, [^0-9].
\s	Whitespace character.
\S	Non-whitespace character.

Table 43. Anchors and other zero-width tests

Sequence	Meaning
^	Start of string, or after any newline if in multiline match mode, /m.
$	End of search string or before a string-ending newline, or before any newline if in multiline match mode, /m.
\b	Word boundary.
\B	Not-word-boundary.

Table 43. Anchors and other zero-width tests (continued)

Sequence	Meaning
(?=...)	Positive lookahead.
(?!...)	Negative lookahead.

Table 44. Mode modifiers

Modifier	Meaning
m	^ and $ match next to embedded line terminators.
i	Case-insensitive match.

Table 45. Grouping, capturing, conditional, and control

Sequence	Meaning
(...)	Group subpattern and capture submatch into \1,\2,... and $1, $2,....
\n	In a regular expression, contains text matched by the nth capture group.
$n	In a replacement string, contains text matched by the nth capture group.
(?:...)	Group subpattern, but do not capture submatch.
...|...	Try subpatterns in alternation.
*	Match 0 or more times.
+	Match 1 or more times.
?	Match 1 or 0 times.
{n}	Match exactly n times.
{n,}	Match at least n times.
{x,y}	Match at least x times but no more than y times.
*?	Match 0 or more times, but as few times as possible.
+?	Match 1 or more times, but as few times as possible.
??	Match 0 or 1 times, but as few times as possible.
{n}?	Match at least n times, but as few times as possible.
{x,y}?	Match at least x times, no more than y times, and as few times as possible.

Pattern-Matching Methods and Objects

JavaScript provides convenient pattern-matching methods in String objects, as well as a RegExp object for more complex pattern matching. JavaScript strings use the backslash for escapes, and therefore any escapes destined for the regular expression engine should be double escaped (e.g., "\\w" instead of "\w"). You can also use the regular expression literal syntax, /pattern/img.

String

Strings support four convenience methods for pattern matching. Each method takes a *pattern* argument, which may be either a RegExp object or a string containing a regular expression pattern.

Methods

search(*pattern*)

>Match *pattern* against the string returning either the character position of the start of the first matching substring or -1.

replace(*pattern, replacement*)

>The replace( ) method searches the string for a match of *pattern* and replaces the matched substring with *replacement*. If *pattern* has global mode set, then all matches of *pattern* are replaced. The replacement string may have $*n* constructs that are replaced with the matched text of the *n*th capture group in *pattern*.

match(*pattern*)

>Match *pattern* against the string returning either an array or -1. Element 0 of the array contains the full match. Additional elements contain submatches from capture groups. In global (g) mode, the array contains all matches of *pattern* with no capture group submatches.

split(*pattern, limit*)

>Return an array of strings broken around *pattern*. If *limit*, the array contains at most the first *limit* substrings broken around *pattern*. If *pattern* contains capture groups, captured substrings are returned as elements after each split substring.

RegExp

Models a regular expression and contains methods for pattern matching.

Constructor

new RegExp(*pattern, attributes*)
/*pattern*/*attributes*
> RegExp objects can be created with either the RegExp() constructor or a special literal syntax /.../. The parameter *pattern* is a required regular expression pattern, and the parameter *attributes* is an optional string containing any of the mode modifiers g, i, or m. The parameter *pattern* can also be a RegExp object, but the *attributes* parameter then becomes required.
>
> The constructor can throw two excpetions. SyntaxError is thrown if *pattern* is malformed or if *attributes* contains invalid mode modifiers. *TypeError* is thrown if *pattern* is a RegExp object and the *attributes* parameter is omitted.

Instance properties

global
> Boolean, if RegExp has g attribute.

ignoreCase
> Boolean, if RegExp has i attribute.

lastIndex
> The character position of the last match.

multiline
> Boolean, if RegExp has m attribute.

source
> The text pattern used to create this object.

Methods

exec(*text*)
> Search *text* and return an array of strings if the search succeeds and null if it fails. Element 0 of the array contains the substring matched by the entire regular expression. Additional elements correspond to capture groups.

If the global flag (g) is set, then lastIndex is set to the character position after the match or zero if there was no match. Successive exec( ) or test( ) calls will start at lastIndex. Note that lastIndex is a property of the regular expression, not the string being searched. You must reset lastIndex manually if you are using a RegExp object in global mode to search multiple strings.

test(*text*)

Return true if the RegExp object matches *text*. The test( ) method behaves in the same way as exec( ) when used in global mode: successive calls start at lastIndex even if used on different strings.

Examples

Example 28. Simple match

```
//Match Spider-Man, Spiderman, SPIDER-MAN, etc.
    var dailybugle = "Spider-Man Menaces City!";

    //regex must match entire string
    var regex = /spider[- ]?man/i;

    if (dailybugle.search(regex)) {
      //do something
    }
```

Example 29. Match and capture group

```
//Match dates formatted like MM/DD/YYYY, MM-DD-YY,...
    var date = "12/30/1969";
    var p =
      new RegExp("(\\d\\d)[-/](\\d\\d)[-/](\\d\\d(?:\\d\\
d)?)");

    var result = p.exec(date);
    if (result != null) {
      var month = result[1];
      var day   = result[2];
      var year  = result[3];
```

Example 30. Simple substitution

```
//Convert <br> to <br /> for XHTML compliance
    String text = "Hello world. <br>";

    var pattern = /<br>/ig;

    test.replace(pattern, "<br />");
```

Example 31. Harder substitution

```
//urlify - turn URL's into HTML links
    var text = "Check the website, http://www.oreilly.com/
catalog/regexppr.";
    var regex =
            "\\b"                      // start at word boundary
        +   "("                        // capture to $1
        +   "(https?|telnet|gopher|file|wais|ftp) :"
                                       // resource and colon
        +   "[\\w/\\#~:.?+=&%@!\\-]+?" // one or more valid chars
                                       // take little as possible
        +   ")"
        +   "(?="                      // lookahead
        +   "[.:?\\-]*"                // for possible punct
        +   "(?:[^\\w/\\#~:.?+=&%@!\\-]"// invalid character
        +   "|$)"                      // or end of string
        +   ")";

    text.replace(regex, "<a href=\"$1\">$1</a>");
```

Other Resources

JavaScript: The Definitive Guide, by David Flanagan (O'Reilly), is a reference for all JavaScript, including regular expressions.

Shell Tools

awk, *sed*, and *egrep* are a related set of Unix shell tools for text processing. *awk* and *egrep* use a DFA match engine, and *sed* uses an NFA engine. For an explanation of the rules behind these engines, see "Introduction to Regexes and Pattern Matching."

This reference covers GNU *egrep* 2.4.2, a program for searching lines of text; GNU *sed* 3.02, a tool for scripting editing commands; and GNU *awk* 3.1, a programming language for text processing.

Supported Metacharacters

awk, *egrep*, and *sed* support the metacharacters and metasequences listed in Tables 46 through 50. For expanded definitions of each metacharacter, see "Regex Metacharacters, Modes, and Constructs."

Table 46. Character representations

Sequence	Meaning	Tool
\a	Alert (bell).	*awk, sed*
\b	Backspace; supported only in character class.	*awk*
\f	Form feed.	*awk, sed*
\n	Newline (line feed).	*awk, sed*
\r	Carriage return.	*awk, sed*
\t	Horizontal tab.	*awk, sed*
\v	Vertical tab.	*awk, sed*
\o*octal*	A character specified by a one-, two-, or three-digit octal code.	*sed*
octal	A character specified by a one-, two-, or three-digit octal code.	*awk*
\x*hex*	A character specified by a two-digit hexadecimal code.	*awk, sed*
\d*decimal*	A character specified by a one, two, or three decimal code.	*awk, sed*
\c*char*	A named control character (e.g., \cC is Control-C).	*awk, sed*
\b	Backspace.	*awk*
metacharacter	Escape the metacharacter so that it literally represents itself.	*awk, sed, egrep*

Table 47. Character classes and class-like constructs

Class	Meaning	Tool
[...]	Matches any single character listed or contained within a listed range.	*awk, sed, egrep*
[^ ...]	Matches any single character that is not listed or contained within a listed range.	*awk, sed, egrep*
.	Matches any single character, except newline.	*awk, sed, egrep*
\w	Matches an ASCII word character, [a-zA-Z0-9_].	*egrep, sed*
\W	Matches a character that is not an ASCII word character, [^a-zA-Z0-9_].	*egrep, sed*
[:*prop*:]	Matches any character in the POSIX character class.	*awk, sed*
[^[:*prop*:]]	Matches any character not in the POSIX character class.	*awk, sed*

Table 48. Anchors and other zero-width testshell tools

Sequence	Meaning	Tool
^	Matches only start of string, even if newlines are embedded.	*awk, sed, egrep*
$	Matches only end of search string, even if newlines are embedded.	*awk, sed, egrep*
\<	Matches beginning of word boundary.	*egrep*
\>	Matches end of word boundary.	*egrep*

Table 49. Comments and mode modifiers

Modifier	Meaning	Tool
flag: i or I	Case-insensitive matching for ASCII characters.	*sed*
command-line option: -i	Case-insensitive matching for ASCII characters.	*egrep*
set IGNORECASE to *non-zero*	Case-insensitive matching for Unicode characters.	*awk*

Table 50. Grouping, capturing, conditional, and control

Sequence	Meaning	Tool
(*PATTERN*)	Grouping.	*awk*
\(*PATTERN*\)	Group and capture sub-matches, filling \1,\2,...,\9.	*sed*
n	Contains the *n*th earlier submatch.	*sed*
...|...	Alternation; match one or the other.	*egrep, awk, sed*
Greedy quantifiers		
*	Match 0 or more times.	*awk, sed, egrep*
+	Match 1 or more times.	*awk, sed, egrep*
?	Match 1 or 0 times.	*awk, sed, egrep*
\{*n*\}	Match exactly *n* times.	*sed, egrep*
\{*n*,\}	Match at least *n* times.	*sed, egrep*
\{*x,y*\}	Match at least *x* times, but no more than *y* times.	*sed, egrep*

egrep

egrep [*options*] *pattern files*

egrep searches *files* for occurrences of *pattern* and prints out each matching line.

Example

```
$ echo 'Spiderman Menaces City!' > dailybugle.txt
$ egrep -i 'spider[- ]?man' dailybugle.txt
Spiderman Menaces City!
```

sed

sed '[*address1*][,*address2*]s/*pattern*/*replacement*/[*flags*]' *files*
sed -f *script files*

By default, *sed* applies the substitution to every line in *files*. Each address can be either a line number or a regular expression pattern. A supplied regular expression must be defined within the forward slash delimiters (/...). If *address1* is supplied, substitution will begin on that line number or the first matching line, and continue until either the end of the file or the line indicated or matched by *address2*.

Two subsequences, & and *n*, will be interpreted in *replacement* based on the results of the match. The sequence & is replaced with the text matched by *pattern*. The sequence *n* corresponds to a capture group (1..9) in the current match.

The available flags are:

n   Substitute the *n*th match in a line, where *n* is between 1 and 512.

g   Substitute all occurrences of *pattern* in a line.

p   Print lines with successful substitutions.

w *file*
    Write lines with successful substitutions to *file*.

Example

Change date formats from MM/DD/YYYY to DD.MM.YYYY.

```
$ echo 12/30/1969' |
  sed 's!\([0-9][0-9]\)/\([0-9][0-9]\)/\([0-9]\{2,4\}\)!\2.\1.\3!g'
```

---

awk

```
awk 'instructions' files
awk -f script files
```

The *awk* script contained in either *instructions* or *script* should be a series of /*pattern*/ {*action*} pairs. The *action* code is applied to each line matched by *pattern*. *awk* also supplies several functions for pattern matching.

Functions

match(*text, pattern*)
    If *pattern* matches in *text*, returns the position in *text* where the match starts. A failed match returns zero. A successful match also sets the variable RSTART to the position where the match started and the variable RLENGTH to the number of characters in the match.

gsub(*pattern*, *replacement*, *text*)
> Substitutes each match of *pattern* in *text* with *replacement* and returns the number of substitutions. Defaults to $0 if *text* is not supplied.

sub(*pattern*, *replacement*, *text*)
> Substitutes first match of *pattern* in *text* with *replacement*. A successful substitution returns 1, and an unsuccessful substitution returns 0. Defaults to $0 if *text* is not supplied.

Example

Create an *awk* file and then run it from the command line.

```
$ cat sub.awk
{
    gsub(/https?:\/\/[a-z_.\\w\/\\#~:?+=&;%@!-]*/,
                "<a href=\"\&\">\&</a>");

    print
}

$ echo "Check the website, http://www.oreilly.com/catalog/
repr" | awk -f sub.awk
```

Other Resources

sed & awk, by Dale Dougherty and Arnold Robbins (O'Reilly), is an introduction and reference to both tools.

Index

Symbols

# comment, 11
$ anchor, 9
(...) parentheses, 11
(?:...) subexpression grouping, 12
(?<name>...) named capture, 12
(?>...) atomic grouping, 12
* greedy quantifier, 12
*+ possessive quantifier, 13
*? lazy quantifier, 13
+ greedy quantifier, 12
++ possessive quantifier, 13
+? lazy quantifier, 13
. (dot), 6
? greedy quantifier, 12
?#... comment, 11
?+ possessive quantifier, 13
?? lazy quantifier, 13
?i mode modifier, 11
?if then | else, 12
[...] character class, 6
[^...] character class, 6
\, 10
\> metacharacter, 10
\1, 11
\A anchor, 9
\B metacharacter, 10
\b metacharacter, 10
\cchar, 6
\D, 6
\d, 6
\G anchor, 9
\num, 5
\p{prop}, 8
\Q...\E (literal text span), 11
\S, 6
\s, 6
\Unum, 5
\unum, 5
\W, 6
\w, 6
\X, 7
\x{num}, 5
\xnum, 5
\Z anchor, 9
\z anchor, 9
^ anchor, 9
| alternation, 12

A

address shortcuts, vi editor, 74
after-match variables, 19

We'd like to hear your suggestions for improving our indexes. Send email to *index@oreilly.com*.

Related Titles Available from O'Reilly

Perl

Advanced Perl Programming

CGI Programming with Perl, *2nd Edition*

Computer Science & Perl Programming: The Best of the Perl Journal

Embedding Perl in HTML with Mason

Games, Diversions, & Perl Culture: The Best of the Perl Journal

Learning Perl, *3rd Edition*

Learning Perl Objects, References and Modules

Mastering Algorithms with Perl

Mastering Perl/Tk

Mastering Regular Expressions, *2nd Edition*

Perl & LWP

Perl & XML

Perl 6 Essentials, *2nd Edition*

Perl CD Bookshelf, *Version 4.0*

Perl Cookbook, *2nd Edition*

Perl Debugger Pocket Reference

Perl for System Administration

Perl Graphics Programming

Perl in a Nutshell, *2nd Edition*

Perl Pocket Reference, *4th Edition*

Perl Template Toolkit

Practical mod_perl

Programming the Perl DBI

Programming Perl, *3rd Edition*

Programming Web Services with Perl

Web, Graphics & Perl/Tk: The Best of the Perl Journal

O'REILLY®

Our books are available at most retail and online bookstores.
To order direct: 1-800-998-9938 • *order@oreilly.com* • *www.oreilly.com*
Online editions of most O'Reilly titles are available at *safari.oreilly.com*

Keep in touch with O'Reilly

1. Download examples from our books

To find example files for a book, go to:
www.oreilly.com/catalog

select the book, and follow the "Examples" link.

2. Register your O'Reilly books

Register your book at *register.oreilly.com*

Why register your books? Once you've registered your O'Reilly books you can:

- Win O'Reilly books, T-shirts or discount coupons in our monthly drawing.
- Get special offers available only to registered O'Reilly customers.
- Get catalogs announcing new books (US and UK only).
- Get email notification of new editions of the O'Reilly books you own.

3. Join our email lists

Sign up to get topic-specific email announcements of new books and conferences, special offers, and O'Reilly Network technology newsletters at:
elists.oreilly.com

It's easy to customize your free elists subscription so you'll get exactly the O'Reilly news you want.

4. Get the latest news, tips, and tools

www.oreilly.com

- "Top 100 Sites on the Web"—PC Magazine
- CIO Magazine's Web Business 50 Awards

Our web site contains a library of comprehensive product information (including book excerpts and tables of contents), downloadable software, background articles, interviews with technology leaders, links to relevant sites, book cover art, and more.

5. Work for O'Reilly

Check out our web site for current employment opportunities:
jobs.oreilly.com

6. Contact us

O'Reilly & Associates
1005 Gravenstein Hwy North
Sebastopol, CA 95472 USA

TEL: 707-827-7000 or 800-998-9938
(6am to 5pm PST)

FAX: 707-829-0104

order@oreilly.com
> For answers to problems regarding your order or our products.
> To place a book order online, visit:
> *www.oreilly.com/order_new*

catalog@oreilly.com
> To request a copy of our latest catalog.

booktech@oreilly.com
> For book content technical questions or corrections.

corporate@oreilly.com
> For educational, library, government, and corporate sales.

proposals@oreilly.com
> To submit new book proposals to our editors and product managers.

international@oreilly.com
> For information about our international distributors or translation queries. For a list of our distributors outside of North America check out:
> *international.oreilly.com/distributors.html*

adoption@oreilly.com
> For information about academic use of O'Reilly books, visit:
> *academic.oreilly.com*

O'REILLY®

Our books are available at most retail and online bookstores.
To order direct: 1-800-998-9938 • *order@oreilly.com* • *www.oreilly.com*
Online editions of most O'Reilly titles are available at *safari.oreilly.com*